The Slaves of Palamau

and Other Writings

MAHASWETA DEVI

Seagull Books
LONDON NEW YORK CALCUTTA

POINTS OF VIEW / V

These essays were originally published in *Dust on the Road* (Seagull Books, 2000), edited and introduced by Maitreya Ghatak.

The footnotes in the present edition have been supplied by the publisher and are not the author's own.

Seagull Books, 2026

ISBN 978 1 80309 704 6

British Library Cataloguing-in-Publication Data
A catalogue record for this book
is available from the British Library

Typeset by Seagull Books, Calcutta, India

What do India's poorest communities reveal about power, land and survival?

In the late 1970s, writer Mahasweta Devi shifted her focus to the lives of marginalized communities in eastern India. Travelling widely and staying with the communities she wrote about, she drew on these firsthand encounters in her writing.

The Slaves of Palamau brings together a selection from her activist prose of the 1980s and early 1990s. With the steady attention that informs her fiction, she examines environmental damange; dispossession and land alienation; and the conditions of landless laborers, sharecroppers, bonded and contract workers, miners and Indigenous communities. Nearly fifty years after India legally abolished bonded labour in 1976, and two decades after the Forest Rights Act recognized forest dwellers' claims to land and livelihood in 2006, the concerns Devi raised remain disturbingly relevant.

MAHASWETA DEVI (1926–2016) was a Bengali writer and activist whose fiction gave voice to Adivasi, Dalit and dispossessed communities. In her fictions and essays, she fused reportage, history and protest, earning enduring acclaim through the Sahitya Akademi, Jnanpith, Padma Vibhushan and Ramon Magsaysay awards.

POINTS OF VIEW

Contents

The Story of Chuni Kotal

Chuni Kotal, a 27-year-old Lodha girl, the first woman graduate among the Lodha–Shabar and Kheria–Shabar of West Bengal, hanged herself on 16 August 1992 at her husband's one-room residence in Kharagpur, a railway town. Chuni's graduation had made the news. The circumstances goading her to despair have aroused public indignation. Calcutta papers have covered the incident widely. The Chief Minister has ordered a judicial inquiry to ascertain the causes that led to her death. This was expected, for West Bengal is a great state for not seeing the naked truth. The reasons that led Chuni, a unique woman, to take her own life are palpable ones and she 'became a victim of sheer injustice and callousness of the university authorities and

---

Economic and Political Weekly, 29 August 1992.

the West Bengal government', according to a press report (*The Statesman*, 23 August 1992).

I have written about the sorry plight of the denotified Lodha–Shabars of West Bengal more than once.[1] The general callousness towards the Lodhas can be seen from the fact that Chuni Kotal, the first woman from a 'primitive' tribe to have passed the Higher Secondary examination, remained unemployed till 1982. That was the year the last major Lodha group-killing took place and by that time I had written often about them, mostly for Bengali dailies.[2] Chuni was appointed Lodha social worker in 1983 at the Jhargram Integrated Tribal Development Project office. From childhood, despite starvation,

1 'Denotified tribes' refers to communities that were historically branded as 'criminal by birth' and 'notified' under colonial Criminal Tribes Acts. These communities were formally denotified after the act's repeal in 1952. West Bengal lists Lodha among its Scheduled Tribes and among its Particularly Vulnerable Tribal Groups.

2 Mahasweta Devi's 1983 EPW reporting counted thirty-four Lodha killings in West Bengal from 1979 to 1982; Das Gupta lists several 1982 attacks, including deaths at Gonua, Jhargram, Shakpara, Khejurkuti, Saro, Baghjhanpa and Chakua. Sanjukta Das Gupta, 'Violence and the Marginalized: The Lodhas of West Bengal', *Cracow Indological Studies* 27 (1) (2025): 257.

working in the fields, having no money to purchase books, she doggedly continued to study. As a social worker she cycled 20–25 km a day and made an extensive survey of the Lodha villages.

All along she continued studying. She had a strong desire to prove to the rest of the world that she, too, could do as well as others, given the opportunity. In 1985 she graduated. In 1987 she was appointed superintendent of Rani Shiromoni Scheduled Caste (SC) and Scheduled Tribe (ST) Girls' Hostel in Medinipur, the district town. She was directly under the district SC and ST Welfare Officer. Her working hours were 24 hours a day, 365 days a year. No holidays, no breaks. If she had to leave the hostel for a few hours or a day, she had to take prior permission from the office, which was very unsympathetic to her.

That she was a Lodha, a hated name in the district, clung to her like a stigma. Some of the hostel staff were dead against her because of her origins. On one occasion her ailing father had to come from the village and stay in her room for a few days as a hospital bed was not available. An officer at the district office accused her of entertaining men in her room. The same thing happened when her brother, who had fractured his leg, came. Once a niece suffering from food poisoning stayed with her. The hostel staff reported her to the office. The officer demanded an explanation. Chuni felt suffocated in the job. Countless times she approached the state government at Writers' Building, pleading for (a) a transfer to her original job and (b) better working conditions. The department remained brutally indifferent. I call the SC and ST Department hunters. Chuni was the quarry.

Matters became worse when Chuni enrolled herself at the local Vidyasagar University as an MSc student in Anthropology. Now weird things began to happen. From the very first day, a certain male professor started abusing her as a member of a criminal tribe, a low-born who had no right to study MSc. The university authorities, the head of the department, did nothing about it. This man was allowed to mark her absent though she was present for days. And Chuni was debarred from sitting for the examination, on grounds of irregular attendance. She lost a year.

The district office made her life miserable for leaving the hostel and going to university. In West Bengal, even after so many years of Left Front rule, the first woman graduate from a very backward tribe was openly abused because of her low caste and birth and nothing was done about it. No one was ashamed and no one cared. Only Chuni suffered. The university authorities, too, are hunters. These anthropologists, nritatva vijnani in Bengali, are head-hunters or nrimunda shikari in Bengali. The second time Chuni sat for her examination, the same male professor gave her low marks. Thus she lost two years.

In desperation she complained and complained and, in 1991, the Education Minister constituted an inquiry commission which consisted of three principals from three district colleges. Throughout, the male faculty member was allowed to refer to the criminal nature of her tribe and to abuse her. The commission just went to sleep.

Chuni felt increasingly desperate and cornered. A tribal girl, she was ill-equipped to fight the enemy, whose ambitions and game plans she was unfamiliar with. Now she also became a victim of the inner politics between the members of the faculty. She did not know the ways of the hunters. The last pressure came from a woman faculty member holding a position of top authority within the department. She had her own axe to grind. She saw an opportunity in the situation and relentlessly pressed Chuni to file a case against the offending male professor. This lady knew that Chuni's relations with the office were bad, that the government had already ordered an inquiry commission and that it would be disastrous for Chuni to file a case at this stage. But she pressed on. This was the ultimate harassment.

In September, the examination was due and Chuni could not afford to incur the displeasure of this woman who professed to be her well-wisher. She had been failed twice already. She felt forced to agree. This must have been the last shove to the abyss.

On 13 August there was a seminar in the university. By that time Chuni knew where she stood. Her working conditions remained the same. She had no hope that the inquiry commission would do justice to her. Now she would have to file a case which would make a further mess of her career. If she did not, the woman faculty member might create problems. She went to the university. Thereafter she weepingly told a few co-students (according to a letter published in a Bengali daily, *Bartaman*, on 25 August 1992) that the male professor had referred to the Lodhas as thieves and robbers, completely out of context. She said that he had threatened her, saying that he would ensure that she not be allowed to sit for the examination in September. She felt that she had wasted two years attending classes without being allowed to sit for the examination, and that, being a Lodha, she should never have dreamt of higher studies. She also said that even though she had made formal complaints to the university authorities, the offenders remained untouched.

One can only imagine what was going on in her mind. By 13 August she had made up her mind. Death was the only way to escape the hunters. On the 14 she went to her husband. They had married in a court in 1990, but due to her job had not been able to stay together. Her husband is a Lodha youth who had passed the Higher Secondary examination and worked in the railway workshop. That Chuni was a graduate and he was not had never created any friction between them. They had been in love with each other from 1981. Manmatha Shabar, the husband, is a simple tribal boy. This time he found Chuni very relaxed, free of tension. They were to leave for Chuni's village, Gohaldihi, on 16 to talk about a formal reception, a post-marriage community feast. On 16, Manmatha left for the workshop at 6.15 a.m. He returned at 10.45 a.m. and found Chuni hanging.

Chuni's death has revealed what West Bengal truly is. Brutal caste and class hostility and persecution have been allowed to continue. The government allowed the district babus to abuse her. Nothing was done to change her working conditions. She was kept a slave of her department. Why not? Was she not a Lodha? Was she not given a job? She should have remained eternally grateful for that. The university authorities did nothing to throw out the caste baiter. And the commission appointed by the government, apparently sleeping so far, suddenly became very active and submitted its report. Only a few days after her death, when there was a hue and cry in the media.

A new kind of hunt. West Bengal has the same caste and class hatred, but the methods are sophisticated and complex; that is the only difference with other states. Chuni's death should not be allowed to go unavenged. The tribals should realize exactly where they stand here. The curse of the babu culture runs in Bengal's veins. West Bengal forces a Chuni Kotal to commit suicide and goes ga-ga over the nauseating display of a 'Sutanuti Utsav', celebrating 300 years of the city of Calcutta.[3]

See the face of West Bengal, now that Chuni has ripped off the mask. A judicial inquiry? Surely

---

3 Sutanuti was one of the old settlement-villages associated with colonial Calcutta, alongside Kalikata and Gobindapur. The city's tercentenary was celebrated in 1990 under the then-conventional Job Charnock/1690 founding narrative; a 2003 Calcutta High Court judgment rejected Charnock as sole founder and 24 August 1690 as the city's birth date.

not. We know that judicial inquiries in West Bengal get lost in a desert of inertia. I think all democratic organizations and people should protest against this naked caste and class oppression and demand a Central Bureau of Investigation inquiry. Is not Chuni's death a pointer to the tribal in India? Well, Bengal has shown its true face.

PS. The university inquiry committee submitted its report in a hurry eight days after Chuni committed suicide. Its finding was that all allegations of harassment made by her were correct. The Ganguly Commission set up to inquire into her suicide found that she committed suicide 'for personal reasons'.[4]

---

4 The Vidyasagar University committee report was issued on 24 August 1992, eight days after Kotal's death, and found her allegations against Falguni Chakraborty of psychological torture on account of her Lodha identity to be 'prima-facie correct'. The Governor ordered the one-man Ganguly Commission on 27 August 1992. Later accounts state that its report treated the death as a 'personal tragedy' and rejected blame against Chakraborty; the report itself has circulated as an unpublished document.

The Chains of Untouchability

By 9 in the morning the heat was almost unbearable. We reached Daltonganj at noon on 30 April. The same evening Rameshwaram, my host, took me to the Domtoli at the riverside. The Koel was dry. Thin streams of water here and there. Men, women and children washing, cleaning utensils and filling earthen pitchers. I want to describe my experience of the Domtoli in some detail as, according to me, this experience is a mirror to Palamau. Crossing Shivaji Maidan, a very prominent place of the small district headquarters town, we turn right, pass Shivala Ghat and the temple, and enter an area of darkness. This is the Domtoli.[1]

Business Standard, 20 May 1981.

1 Toli means a hamlet or neighbourhood; Domtoli here denotes the Dom settlement.

I saw that the surrounding area had electricity, but the Domtoli, even the road before it, had not a single electric lamppost. The dwellers of the toli came in ones and twos to meet us, and an old woman, Tetri-mausi, greeted us with a string of abusive words, 'Now they have come for votes. No, we are not interested. Please leave us in peace.' Rameshwaram, in vigorous local dialect, silenced her. Oh, so it was Rameshwaram who had come. Well, he was okay because he had no power, nor had he ever promised them anything. He could be trusted. But people who promised them succour from eternal misery could not be trusted. Not any more. A khatiya was dragged out, bidis and khaini changed hands. We drank water. Talks began.

The Domtoli is situated on government land secured for them by Kamala Prasad Vakil, a former member of parliament, long ago. Idris Khan and Laksman Babu Khainiwala have usurped their land and raised buildings on it. A civil case is going on. A government-appointed pleader is handling their case. No, they do not know the name of the pleader, nor anything about the development of the case. Why? Because none of them are literate. Are there not schools? Yes, why not? There were Madhya Vidyalaya on Shivala Ghat, a primary school, and Girivar High School on Shivaji Maidan, both very near. But Harijan children are not allowed there. Once the daughter of a headmaster visited the toli urging them to send their children to school. Her father first wanted Rs 10 for each student. This they were ready to pay. But then the headmaster refused to admit them. So the children remain illiterate.

The toli has 50 to 60 huts and 200 residents. The Doms are municipal employees. They sweep the streets, carry night soil and remove dead animals from the streets, for which they receive Rs 2 per animal. Their salary on paper is Rs 227 a month but they only get Rs 100. 'What to do, Mataji? Everyone wants and demands bribes.' They are allowed only 15 days' leave a year. The women get maternity leave not for three months, as per rule, but for a month and 10 days. Previously maternity leave was granted for a month and 15 days. They have to pay a bribe if they are absent. How do they manage to survive on Rs 100? Why, there are moneylenders to oblige them. The rate of interest is very high. The town of Daltonganj has five police stations and 600 municipal employees who are Doms.

Yes, the municipality issues uniforms in their names, but they never receive them. Only once during the floods were they given Rs 55 per head, a sari or a dhoti each and some sattu or khichri for two or three days. Yes, they are untouchables. During election-campaign time, often the candidates do not come to them. They have to go to the various candidates before sunrise or after sunset. To see an untouchable face to face would be inauspicious indeed. One kaiti and a mochi, rich persons both, have failed them too. The mochi took the four big bundles of clothes, rice and atta issued in their names for himself. Once his sister had beaten up Tetri-mausi.

Despite repeated appeals and promises they still have not been given electricity. During a wedding they borrow it from their upper-caste neighbours. No drinking water for them. The river bed is their latrine, river water their drinking water. During the monsoons, they purify the muddy Koel water with alum and drink it. There are five prostitute centres nearby. The women of the toli are molested, too. Urmila's mother Dhanmania was killed by two local toughs who entered her hut demanding women. Tetri's sister was run over by a tractor and killed. But the person concerned gave a bribe of Rs 1,000 and nothing came of the police case. Of course, they are not allowed inside the temples. Usually they do puja inside their huts. On special occasions they go to the temple priests and place money on the earth, which the priest purifies with Ganga water before accepting.

The toli has five castes living there. I have spoken about the Doms. The Bhuiya men carry loads and their women break rocks at Rs 3 for eight hours' labour. The Chamars make shoes.

Their women sever the navel cord of the newborn, give oil massages to the infant and the mother as long as they remain 'impure' owing to janmashoucha[2] and receive 50 paise per day. They get some bakshish after the 'unclean' period is over. Kaharas work where they can; Kurmi men sell gram; their women clean utensils.

The ostracized existence of the Domtoli reveals the pulse of the place. Daltonganj is a small town and these social injustices go on openly there, and no one is concerned. Dr Ambedkar's birthday celebration takes place somewhere, official institutions for the upliftment of Harijans exist, but the untouchables are left untouched. The idea that Scheduled Caste and Tribe people are meant to serve the upper castes has entered the bones of the landowners, forest contractors and bureaucracy. The two all-India Communist Party offices are present in Daltonganj, but they, too, remain uninterested. This explains why the downtrodden never stand up and fight for their

2 Janmashoucha is the ritual impurity associated with childbirth.

legitimate rights. They have learnt that in order to survive, it is safer to suffer silently, because no one is bothered about them. We can take part in international affairs, our Aryabhattas and other satellites may reach outer space, but no one in India can raise the untouchables of the innumerable Domtolis of Palamau to the status of free individuals.

Why Independence? Why say we are a free nation? What right have we to do so? After so many years of this Independence, we see Tagore's words come true. Our untouchables have made us untouchables too, for we have allowed this curse of untouchability to flourish and stay.

The Slaves of Palamau

They came from 50 villages in the district of Palamau, Bihar[1]—men, women and children, some of them in their mother's arms—trudging into the district town of Daltonganj. All of them shared a common bond; they were all bandhuas or bonded labourers. There were 2,000 of them who have not yet been officially identified by the district administration for, it seems, the administration has one of its eyes shut. The official figure put out is 1,014. In private conversation, however, district officials themselves consider the official figure an absurdity. The administration depends upon the

Sunday, 3–9 July 1983.

1 Palamau was in Bihar when this essay appeared. Jharkhand, comprising districts formerly in southern Bihar, was created on 15 November 2000; present-day Palamu is in north-western Jharkhand, and Daltonganj is officially Medininagar.

sarpanchs and the mukhias of the villages, and in Palamau these village chiefs are those to whom the labourers are bonded.

It is totally inconceivable that a bandhua can actually come forward and declare himself to the district administration, defying the near-almighty Rajput or brahman who has, over centuries, exploited and used him as a slave. To unite the bonded labourers and urge them to come forward jointly and fight against exploitation, needs courage. Such a task is best achieved by individuals or organizations with dedication. Palamau is fortunate to have the editor of *Ishumaan*, Rameshwaram, a true friend of the bonded labourers. It was through his efforts that Mughal Bhuiya, a bandhua from Semra, participated in the Bandhua Choupal organized by Swami Agnivesh in Delhi in 1981.[2] This year, on 1 May 1983, Rameshwaram took a step forward by organizing a meeting of the bonded labourers in Daltonganj under the aegis

2 Bandhua Mukti Morcha means Bonded Labour Liberation Front. Swami Agnivesh founded and chaired the organization, which became closely associated with campaigns against bonded labour.

of *Ishumaan* and the Palamau (Bihar) Bandhua Mukti Morcha (PBMM).

The PBMM is often referred to as 'our samiti' by the bonded labourers. In 1981, I saw with my own eyes what it is to be a bandhua when I hitch-hiked to Semra, a predominantly bandhua village, along with Rameshwaram and a few other people (see 'Back to Bondage'). The Semra landowners lived in the village proper while the bonded labourers lived in scattered groups on surrounding hillocks. On one such hillock we celebrated May Day by forming a Bandhua Samiti. At that time we had seen how bonded labourers who had been liberated by the landlords had not benefited at all. The reason was the social structure of Palamau, which, simply put, is medieval. The upper-caste landowners cannot and will not touch a plough although they own the land. Society is sharply divided between landowners and bonded labourers.

Located on the western border of Bihar, Palamau lies in the north-western part of the Chhotanagpur plateau. At one time the district boasted of great jungles. Today, the jungles are largely destroyed and the district can be described as dry upland. The district is predominantly rural and 88.6 per cent of the working population depends on agriculture. Like other districts where the incidence of bonded labour is high, the district has a very high concentration of Scheduled Caste (SC) and Scheduled Tribe (ST) population (44.53 per cent as against a total of 22.86 per cent in Bihar). There is practically no industry worth the name and the main commerce is around jungle products like lac. 'Palamau is the most backward district in a very backward state.'[3]

But this most backward district of a very backward state had, in 1857, risen in revolt against the joint forces of the jagirdars[4] and the British. The poor and the downtrodden had risen

---

3 T. Vijayendra, Maitreya Ghatak, and Vijay Rukmini Rao, 'Rehabilitation of Bonded Labour in India: Study of Two Cases', *Human Futures* (Delhi), Winter 1981.

4 A jagirdar held a jagir, a land or revenue assignment; a zamindar was a landholder or revenue intermediary, though the precise powers and usages varied by region and period.

in an armed revolt which had reached formidable dimensions. In Palamau it was a civil uprising, not military. But those are tales of the past. The heroes of the uprising, Nilambar and Pitambar, do not have institutions named after them. In Palamau, today's ministers have colleges named after them. Even the Chief Minister of the state has a school named after him. Their names are mightier than the heroes who fought the British. Characteristically, the ruined fortress-palace of the Palamau kings stands neglected, without even a plaque. The revolt was crushed, the fighters were hanged, the 'loyalists' were granted big jagirs. The hereditary zamindars of Palamau, the brahmans and the Rajputs, are mostly descendants of the loyalists of yesterday. After 1857, the zamindars and the moneylenders usurped all the land. The kamiauti–seokia or the bandhua system or debt-bondage system was born. How callously the district administration 'identifies' the number of bandhuas will be clear from the following: 'In the 1920–21 settlement, a survey of such kamias was taken and their number was estimated at over 60,000 . . .'[5] It is only natural that the number has increased over the last six decades. It is no use to have only a thousand identified and rehabilitated. What about the unidentified thousands who are getting into fresh bondage?

The samiti did not sit idle after 1 May 1981. The more courageous among the bandhuas themselves came forward and contacted fellow bandhuas. It is well known that the liberated bandhuas face a lot of hardships—the landowners refuse to employ them—yet they are happy to be out of bondage. It is these people who made the choupal (meeting) a success.

The choupal began at 10 in the morning of 1 May at the local town hall named after Mahatma Gandhi. It was, perhaps, the first time that Harijans, Muslims and tribals entered the hall. The bandhuas themselves were on the stage. They conducted the first session, addressing the gathering. For people living in subhuman

5 Vijayendra, Ghatak, and Rao, 'Rehabilitation of Bonded Labour in India'.

conditions, they showed great courage and clarity of thought. As they talked, the full horror of the misery of bondage became increasingly clear. Tetri Bhuyin, a woman from Pathalgarhwa, recounted how she had once borrowed Rs 12 from Chamru Sahu and how she had been working for him for the last 10 years for a meal a day and some food grain only. Sahu had refused to release her, she said. Under the bandhua system, all over India, a man borrows some money—it might be for food, a death in the family, hunger, sickness, a daughter's marriage, anything. The borrower then puts his thumb impression on a piece of paper and thus becomes debt-bonded. From then on he will work for the moneylender for an extremely low wage till the debt is repaid with interest. In reality, however, the debt is never repaid, for the interest goes on mounting. The process of debt-repayment thus continues for generations.

Tetri Bhuyin was cruelly beaten by her owner (she is nothing but a slave) for attending the choupal, yet she had come. Mangru Bhuiya spoke for the 22 participants of Karso village. 'My malik (master) threatened to kill us if we came to the choupal. But brother Mogol Bhuiya of Semra put courage into us, so we came. The sarpanchs and the mukhias usurp everything meant for us. See that they don't,' he warned. Chelan Munda, a non-bandhua, Birju Bhuiya, a bandhua liberated by Rameshwaram the editor, Mogol—all had helped the bandhuas. Then stood up Mohammed Kasim, an old man, to narrate his story. He is one of the 32 bandhuas owned by Taramoni Singh of village Solay, under Patan police station. 'My father had once borrowed Rs 10 or Rs 15 from Jagga Singh, Taramoni's father. He died after 45 years of bondage. I, too, have been a bandhua for the last 32 years. Between father and son we have given 77 years of our lives, yet the debt remains unpaid. Why tell me that the law against bonded labour has been passed? My malik does not know—who will tell him?'[6]

6 The Bonded Labour System (Abolition) Ordinance, 1975, was promulgated on 24 October 1975; the Act that replaced it was deemed to have come into force on 25 October 1975. It abolished bonded labour, discharged bonded labourers from obligations to render such labour, and extinguished bonded debts.

There were others, too. Panchu Bhuiya's father had borrowed Rs 35 from Taramoni. Between father and son they had been bandhuas for 60 years. Suleman and Sujait have been bandhuas for 40 years for debts of Rs 20 and Rs 40 respectively. Tabrumal borrowed Rs 15, worked for 20 years, went blind and the legacy of bondage was inherited by his son who has been a bandhua for the past 16 years. Gora Mian's father borrowed 18 kg of rice and worked for 21 years to repay it. Then Gora took over from him. He has been a bandhua for the last 27 years. Taramoni owns the above-mentioned bandhuas. He is believed to be a scholar and a learned man. He has 'bequeathed' the bandhuas to his son Pitambar Lallu.

The bandhuas of Palamau are given names like kamia, seokia, harwaha, charwaha, etc. Among them the dharumaru is in a special category. The malik grabs any person and forces him or her to become a bandhua. Sachita Panre of Bhandar (under police station Bisrampur) has kept Tetri Bhuyin and her family as dharumarus for two generations. In the same village Amresh Panre has forced Bideshi Bhuiya to become his dharumaru. Amresh has also had Bideshi's meagre homestead surveyed and usurped. The Panres of Bhandar are especially powerful because Badri Panre is the sarpanch through whom government schemes for the bandhuas will be implemented if ever they are released. The Rs 4,000 package scheme for each bandhua family comes through the sarpanch, no one else.

Badri Panre, the sarpanch of Bisrampur, according to most of the labourers, is a very cruel malik. He is one of the many maliks who demand absurd sums for releasing the bandhuas. Nanku Bhuiya said, 'My ancestors borrowed Rs 130 from Badri Panre's ancestors. First my grandfather, then my father . . . who can count how many years? . . . I have been working for him for 30 years. Today, the sarpanch demands Rs 400 for my release.' Badri Panre refuses to release Joshini Devi, who borrowed Rs 200 from the sarpanch to fight off starvation five or six years ago. Since then, she has been working for him with her husband and father-in-law.

The list before me is long. I have noted down the names of a few and I find, even from this random sample-list, 74 people who have been bonded in the last five years. It is several years since the Bonded Labour System (Abolition) Ordinance was passed.

In faraway Kachan it was almost a different story. Some bandhua families live there in abject poverty. Why do they become bonded? And why do the non-bonded poor envy those in bondage? Because the bandhuas get meals from the maliks, even if it be of inferior quality, while the non-bonded just starve. The bandhuas of Mahuadanr do not even have a well for drinking water. There are schools, ration shops and health centres but there is nothing for them. Even the land on which their homes stand is owned by the maliks.

Anyone who thinks that the zamindari system has been abolished should visit Palamau. There is no such word as land-ceiling. The poor say they live on the zamindar's land, yet Bihar passed the land reform bill in the 1950s. An eight-year-old child became a bonded labourer in Kachan. The administration is not interested; neither are the political parties.

The miracle had been achieved. The bandhuas of Palamau had united to make the choupal a success. And Tetri was not afraid any more. From now on the bandhuas themselves would be able to assert their rights, with a little guidance and some assistance. And there were people who would willingly help.

A Countryside Slowly Dying

A visit to Singbhum was long under contemplation,[1] so the invitation to attend a meeting, or sammelan, of the tribals of Rajenka and other villages was most welcome. The ACC factory of Jhikpani is causing much distress in the locality because cement dust carried by the wind is ruining crops and vegetation. The sammelan was organized by a committee constituted of people belonging to the Jharkhand Mukti Morcha, Kolhan Raksha Sangh, United Mineral Workers' Union, Mahila Samaj of Chakradharpur, Roro asbestos miners and nearby villages. The approach to Jhikpani from Chaibasa was marked by a changing landscape.

Sunday, 3–9 July 1983.

1 *Economic and Political Weekly*, 5 March 1983.

The fields lay barren and grey under layers of accumulated cement dust. The trees looked ghostly, the leaves hanging listless, heavy with cement dust. In the weekly haat at Jhikpani the air was hazy with grey dust. Cement dust fell relentlessly upon everyone and everything. Within minutes we, too, were covered with cement dust. The tribals bought and sold, going about their business without concern. The open sheds selling liquor were doing brisk business.

In the afternoon we went and saw the places nearby. Rajenka village is one of the worst sufferers. It lies permanently enveloped in cement dust. There were several of us on the team. What we saw defies description.

Big lakes mirror the sky and it is soothing to the eye to see water after traversing a scorched countryside. These are not natural lakes, though they look like nature's gift to a dry and savaged landscape. They are abandoned mines. According to the Metalliferous Mines Regulations, they are illegal. 'Shaft and open cast workings temporarily or permanently out of use and any place in or about an excavation which is dangerous shall be completely filled up or kept securely fenced', says the rule. And, in the same chapter, 'Before a mine is abandoned or the working thereof discontinued, the owner, agent or manager shall cause the top or entrance of every shaft, incline or other opening into the mine to be fenced by a structure of permanent character sufficient to effectively prevent persons falling into or entering the same'.

The huge water tanks around Jhikpani are abandoned mines which have not been filled up. Even a fence or a permanent structure around them will not help solve the peculiar problem caused by the huge pits. The surrounding area consists of agricultural fields. It is also a non-irrigated area. Rainwater is the only source of relief for the peasantry. The water which is so soothing to the eye is actually stolen water. During the rains the rainwater flows into the pits, leaving the fields dry, where enough irrigation can help vegetation growth. This was amply proved by the greenery around the rural health centre. The menace is very real and the peasants are justifiably aggrieved about it. The steep drop to water level was almost vertical. It looked as if only Jim Corbett's ghoorals could tackle the descent. Yet we found vegetable patches covering the same vertical landline. We crossed the fields and tanks and reached the main road towards the plant. Open drains on both sides carry cement dust to another pit. The day is not distant when this pit, too, will be filled up with cement waste. In Singbhum district a 50-km belt of limestone extends from Chaibasa to Jagannathpur.

ACC has about 19 cement factories in India and Jhikpani might be the oldest. It employs about 2,000 workers in the factory and the quarry, consisting of about 800 permanent and 1,200 casual labourers. Are the casual labourers recruited by contractors? I don't know. And while all the unskilled labourers are tribals, only about 20 per cent of the skilled labourers are from the tribes. Not a happy picture at all. The Jhikpani plants produce something like 7,20,000 tonnes per year. Production has gone up in the last 30 years, but the number of labourers remains static. The factory runs in three shifts, round the clock.

The twin giant chimneys emanate cement exhaust. My informant told me that every day about 700 tonnes of cement dust are released from the chimneys. The term he used was 'cement gas'. I don't know his method of calculation. The difference between crude limestone and cement, both measured by weight? Whatever it is, the dust menace is a real threat. A 10-mile radius area around the factory looks like a vast nightmare. Cement dust, accumulated and hardened by night moisture, kills vegetation slowly. Trees wither, paddy, lentil and jowar plants give up and die, unable to survive in soil hardened by cement dust. The peasants and casual majdoors inhale cement dust and die of tuberculosis. It has never been properly investigated whether the tuberculosis found in the area is caused by silicosis or not. A fair and impartial survey of tubercular deaths could be revealing. The workers in the factory and the people living around suffer. The cattle suffer, too. When the health of humans is treated with callousness, who thinks of animals? Cattle inhale cement dust, contract tuberculosis and die. The Singbhum lifescape is one of savage indifference.

The Metalliferous Mines Regulations 1961, amended up to 1980, have eight clauses on dust control in another chapter (precautions against danger from fire, dust, gas and water). All the rules are ignored with supreme contempt. A proper exhaust system will control the dust menace, but why install it at so much cost when 2,000 workers can produce 2,000 tonnes of cement per day and when every day casual labour queues up at the factory gate, begging to be taken on for the day?

The sammelan was held in the open before a beautiful pavilion of split bamboo covered with leafy branches. Peasants and workers of the area had united in hundreds. Most of them were tribals, largely of the Ho tribe. The Ho people of Singbhum are a mighty race—both the young and the old had come. A significant section of the gathering was non-tribal. Rasiklal Honaga, the mukhia of Dokatta panchayat in Tonto block, said with quiet despair that fields previously yielding 15 maunds of paddy per acre were now yielding five. Cement dust affected his panchayat, crop failure was an everyday experience and cattle died of eating dust-laden leaves and grass.

Moreover, the ACC plant was expanding and usurping villagers' lands in a most arbitrary manner. The villagers never know how much land the company will take, or whose. The ACC does not bother to take the permission of the owner of the land. It just says that money against the land has been deposited with the treasury. In the past, it used to consult the mukhias, mundas, mankis, sarpanchs.[2] Now it does not.

Land grabbing by the ACC goes on, seemingly in an illegal manner. Kandwa, Rajenka and Dokatta are already in the acquired area. Nimidh, Kudahati, Jorapokar, Barajhikpani and Dodonga are under threat. Since the area under

---

2 In Kolhan's manki–munda system, a munda is a village head; a manki oversees a cluster of villages.

the factory falls under the limestone belt, the villagers have to give up their land so that ACC can increase cement production. According to the rules, leases have to be renewed every 30 years and the landowners properly compensated. Acquiring tribal land is illegal but it can be done under the cover of law when a factory needs expansion. Land is being taken forcibly and the cultivator harassed by the police if he tills his own land. Surprisingly, he is told that he is cultivating ACC land.

In this acquirement of land lies hidden the promise of a job in the factory. It became clear when a casual labourer showed an appeal by several casual labourers, venting their grievances. Their land was taken over, but no compensation was paid. Promise of work was given but they were kept on as casual labourers at the factory for years with 8–10 days of work a month. They did not enjoy earned leave or sick leave benefits, nor did they receive gur, soda, hats or boots. They were not being made permanent.

Gumia Shundi of Baihatu village was a discharged labourer of the Roro mines. He was very vocal and spoke most impressively. After two deaths in the Roro mines there was a 48-hour gherao. The authorities gave assurances about adopting preventive measures against accidents and undertaking asbestos dust control. After that, seven workers were discharged, including Gumia. His livelihood now depended upon gathering and selling firewood. But life in the villages was hazardous. The police were seizing paddy, too. So the villagers had to keep paddy hidden in the jungles. Because of the JMM movement the police had set fire to the village of Sangajatha. Gumia squarely condemned the mankis and mundas for their inaction against the asbestos dust hazard. (These mundas are not necessarily Munda tribals. The village heads are known as mundas, too.)

The figures I have mentioned have been collected from the people working in the factory. It baffles me why there has never been a militant movement against forcible land usurpation by the ACC, the cement dust hazard and negligence over filling up the abandoned mines. The factory has unions. The Jhikpani plant of the ACC is the other example of the dubious role of the established trade unions. The abandoned pits converted into water reservoirs can be solidly walled around so as to stop rainwater from pouring or seeping in. The water can be used for irrigation purposes, too. But the cement dust hazard? Sunil Sengupta, another member of our team, said from his European experience that cement factories were common but such health and cultivation hazards caused by cement dust were uniquely Indian. I thought of the limestone quarries I had seen between Bilaspur and Rajnandgaon in Madhya Pradesh. Many more factories and a slow death of the countryside. It is easier, in Singbhum, to kill and terrorize the ordinary people with the law on your side. The ACC is too powerful to abide by the law.

On the morning of 30 January we had gone to Serengsi Ghati where the Ho people had fought the British in the 19th century. We left the jeep at Serengsi village and covered the distance on foot.

The jungles were beautiful, with wild plums ripe under the sun and early palash flowers heralding the spring. A favourite haunt of the elephants, the area was in the interior. The tiny rivulet, Charna, accompanied us. Three old villagers led the way. They still remembered the story of the battle handed down by their ancestors. The tribal king's war-cry could be heard from a place which was named Rajenka to commemorate the event. A flat stone under a mowa tree marked the line of advance by the tribals. The atmosphere was charged with the past of a people who still record everything in the mind, not on paper. Nor do they believe in commemorating things our way. I asked them to keep a stone plaque at Serengsi village with the notification of the battle. A quick dip in the Charna brought the past even nearer. Once the rocky and steep banks of the Charna had witnessed a fierce battle where the mighty British had fought and lost. Those were the days the brave Kolhans dreamt of. The forests were primeval. No 'social forestry' as one sees in West Bengal. No eucalyptus plantations with the forest floor bare of undergrowth, as one sees in Jhargram. Here the sal, arjun, sidha, kusum and palash crowded the skyline. The undergrowth was undisturbed. I saw basakas, anantamul and other medicinal plants. The sight of Ho women pumping water from newly sunk tubewells was a pleasant surprise. The Gua firing and the accompanying stir had moved the administration a little and the tubewells were sunk after that.[3] That's what they told me.

From Serengsi we had come to Jhikpani. The grey countryside is still a nightmarish memory. Who can save the countryside from a slow and inevitable death? What is going to happen to the hapless villagers so wrongly and cruelly deprived of their land? Only the people of Singbhum can work out a solution with a continuous and consistent movement, not a merely sporadic and thunderous one. Under whose leadership? I do not know.

---

3 The 'Gua firing' refers to the 8 September 1980 confrontation at Gua in Singhbhum district, reported at the time as leaving four policemen and eleven Adivasis dead.

Contract Labour or Bonded Labour?

On 16 May, *The New Republic of Ranchi* published an account of some bonded labourers rescued from Sasaram after they had served their master for 22 years under subhuman conditions. They had been lured away to Sasaram with promises of 'good jobs', kept in captivity and made to break stones and blast rocks.

The bonded labour system was formally abolished in November 1975. Following that, a new system of recruiting bonded labourers was very quickly introduced in the bonded labour areas. Since their ex-masters would not give them work and since little was done by the state governments towards their rehabilitation, the landless ex-bonded labourers were in acute distress. Now came the agents of various masters

---

Economic and Political Weekly, 6 June 1981.

to lure them away to faraway places with promises of good jobs. Once they reached these places, they found themselves in a worse form of bondage.

The young ones are waiting for the inevitable dalal to come one day and take them away. Many are going. They hear of their good fortune in the weekly haat. The masters are good, give two square meals a day. Even the young ones are not against becoming a kamia or a seokia. 'What to do? There is nothing else for the likes of us.' The land given to the freed bonded labourers is uncultivable. The good land is held by the master, though the ownership paper is in the freed labourer's name. There is no water for drinking or irrigation; no chance of being employed by government agencies for road-repairing, timber-felling, etc. Though Palamau is a labour-surplus and poverty-stricken district, outside labour is brought in for such work. Forsaken by the government and society, these people, in order to stay alive, enter debt-bondage. They do not have any alternative.

I stared at the face of the young boy. What would he become? A seokia, a kamia, a jonwar? A harwaha, a charwaha? Would he receive some tanr, dry palhatu land? Palhatu land is not given away to the cattle grazer or charwaha, who just cultivates it as long as he is in service. I have spelt out the background in some detail in order to stress the conditions in which poor Adivasis, Muslims and Scheduled Caste people are recruited by the labour contractors.[1]

Some of my friends in the villages and forests are very unusual, but Purnendu Mazoomdar is in a class by himself. I am sure that there are very few like him anywhere. His is a household name in the poor villages of Tamar, Bundu, Torpa, Khunti, Chakradharpur, Monoharpur, Gua—over a wide region covering the two districts of Ranchi and Singbhum. He is with the poor tribals and non-tribals in their struggle to gain their forest rights, in their fight

---

1 These are local terms for forms of attached agrarian or pastoral labour; harwaha and charwaha denote, respectively, a ploughman and a cattle-grazer. The 1976 Act's illustrative list of customary forced-labour systems includes kamiya and sewakia.

with the factory and mine owners against prolonged lockouts, in their battle to cling to the land others snatch away from them. Short, animated and simple, this middle-aged man speaks many tribal languages and is considered to be the tribal's true friend. He starves with the tribals, stays with them and walks hundreds of miles to visit his people when they are in distress. He is also the general secretary of the Mineral Workers' Union, Chakradharpur.

A few months ago he came to me with Laru Jonko, a remarkable Ho woman. She was the president of the Mahila Samiti of Chiriburu and had just succeeded in tracing several Adivasi girls who were missing from the interior villages of Singbhum. These girls were working in brick kilns around Calcutta. The story was revealing.

The brick-kiln owners of West Bengal are mostly from north Bihar. This practice of recruitment of Adivasi labour must be quite old. Adivasi women, ex-concubines of the kiln owners, are sent to remote villages. The link railway stations are Chaibasa, Sonwa, Pendrasali and

Chakradharpur. These recruiting women are called sardars. They go to the village haats and lure young girls with tales of good jobs near the magic city of Calcutta.

Chiriburu is the place where the Orissa Cement Company has a quartzite mine. This mine has been under illegal lockout by the owners since 8 March 1979 and 2,000 Adivasi rejas have been starving as a result.[2] Gua leaped into the limelight in 1980. This is the region where militant and indomitable tribals and non-tribals are fighting for their rights to the forest and the land. Relentless police and military repression goes on here. After the Gua firing, ploughs have been broken, cattle and poultry seized, food grains destroyed; women have lost izzat and huts have been razed to the ground. Women can survive on jungle roots and fruits but they need money to buy clothes. So it has been easy for the sardars to collect a willing batch of girls, bribe the police, railway police and the political parties, and bring the girls to Calcutta.

---

2 Reja is a regional term for a woman labourer, here especially a recruited brick-kiln worker.

Each kiln employs 200 to 400 rejas, and each sardar receives Rs 30–40 commission for each reja, so it is easy to understand that the lure of ready money is too much for the sardar. Why does the sardar do it, being a tribal herself? I have said that the sardars are one-time concubines of the kiln owners, and close association with the owners corrupts these women. They are usually despised by their own folk. They become virtual outcasts.

I find, from the written account of Purnendu Mazoomdar, that the women sardars, Sona Jonko and Nandi Jamuda, have supplied 34 rejas to the kilns of Magra in West Bengal from the villages of Komay, Ichakuti and Banka, all under Chakradharpur police station. Two male sardars, Dibru Lohar and Madru Angari, have supplied, to the same kiln, five girls from the villages of Sagipi, Shengao and Otuoti under the same police station.

The kiln owners or bhatta-maliks begin by buying paddy land from poor peasants to build the kiln. Since the adjoining paddy fields are ruined by constant use by the rejas as passage to the bhatta, the owners ultimately sell them to the bhatta-malik. The rejas receive one token or tikli for carrying 10 unbaked bricks over 300 to 400 yards. The same payment is received for carrying 10 baked or pucca bricks. For kutcha or unbaked bricks, 20 tokens mean Re 1. One rupee for carrying 200 kutcha bricks. For pucca bricks, 44 tokens mean Re 1. One rupee for carrying 440 pucca bricks. The rejas cannot earn more than Rs 4–5 per day. Children aged 10–12 constitute 25 per cent of the total labour strength. Where an adult reja earns Rs 25–30 a week, a child earns Rs 10–15. However, an adult actually receives only Rs 15 per week and a child Rs 10. An adult can buy 4 kilos of rice per week and a child 3 kilos. Rice with salt is their only food. Do they get the rest of their wages when they go home? No, never. Paupers they come and paupers they go. Yet they come again the next year. Why?

Sardars who have become too recognized do not approach the prospective rejas directly, but send sub-agents. They explore fresh areas. The rejas who have had a bad experience are easily misled when a new agent approaches them and promises better working conditions. The last and ultimate decider of their fate, of course, is the state government's total apathy towards them. 1980 was a drought year, so there was remission of land tax. This year, tax arrears are being collected with much zulm. Cause enough to drive these people to desperate measures. We are talking of a region where Rs 30 a month is considered a handsome income for an adult and an income of Rs 20 per month is nearer reality. The villagers have land, but it is unproductive and dry. Villagers living in the neighbourhood of a town can sell firewood in the town market. Those living in the remote interior cannot. So they go to the sardars. The sardars prefer young unmarried girls. They are better workers and good for sale.

They force these young girls to sleep with the owners, the supervising staff, the truck drivers, khalasis and local mastaans. Anyone who refuses to cooperate is first locked up in a room, beaten and then seared with a hot iron. It is usual to make a girl drink heavily and then send her for the master's pleasure. A young Ho girl, aged 16, has been compelled to become the aurat of an aged kiln owner at Gajipara in 24 Parganas, West Bengal. She is from the village Dharamsai under Chakradharpur police station.

In politically conscious West Bengal these rejas are denied a minimum wage, medical facilities, maternity leave or any kind of leave, and, of course, the right to form a union. There is no attendance or pay register, identity card or employment card. The set-up is very cruel and very cunning. It is impossible for an outsider to break into the fortress of the bhattas. The rejas cannot leave the bhatta or talk to anyone without the prior permission of the owner. The sardar never lets them out of her sight. A close guard is kept on them.

These unfortunate beings live in jhopdis worse than pig holes. There are no sanitary arrangements, nor any drinking water where they work through the summer days. The kiln is closed with the onset of the monsoons and the rejas are sent home.

Male recruiting sardar Ponka Gagrai of village Dhipasai, Chakradharpur police station, avoids entering village Bari for fear of a possible encounter with Budhu Oihar and Kanklo Gop. He had taken away Budhu's daughter Pechi and Kanklo's daughter Jema six years ago to Patna and the two girls have not come back ever since. From Kharswan and Sagipi villages he supplied 100 labourers to Bakhtiarpur for a farm owner. In November 1980 he took seven girls from Sagipi to Benares. From Kharswan he supplied Shilai Bodra and 34 more girls to a kiln owner of Ayodhya. Kachi Daroga, P.O. Jatla, Patna, received 30 to 35 girls. All these girls are young and many of them physically attractive. Not all of them will come back after the brick-making season is over. A mother sings to the baby on her lap:

> My Bali could live on forest fruits,
> My Bali could live on jungle roots;
> But trees, alas, do not saris grow,
> So to the bhatta my Bali had to go.
> My Bali had to go.

Where are the Jagtas and Balis and Charibas? If you ask the parents, they say simply that life was too hard, survival was threatened, the bhattas called out to them and they left.

I have spoken of West Bengal. What happens in Bihar? Bihar, to me, is the true mirror of India. Bihar has everything in plenty. Even bonded and contract labourers.

The Oraon, Ho and Munda tribals meet the needs of hundreds of kilns on the Ganges, at Muzaffarpur, Samastipur, Bhojpur, Begusarai, Monghyr, Purnea, Gaya, Patna and Chhapra. The coolie jhopdis are within the towns and cities, yet the tribals stay imprisoned there, closely guarded by the muscle-men of the owners. Theirs is a medieval existence far beyond the reach of statutory labour law benefits and democratic rights.

The recruiting end is in the hands of the sardars. They take the munshis (agents / managers) of the owners to their villages and keep them carefully concealed. August and September, the monsoon months, are the worst for the tribals. This is the time when they are starving, totally helpless.

The munshi and the sardar arrange grand feasts and invite the local youth. Through them they get to know of the whereabouts of girls. Then they make the rounds with ready cash in hand. The munshi pays dadan or advance money to the parents of the girls. Once the parents accept Rs 100–150 from the munshi, the girls become contract-bound. They cannot refuse to go and work. In the bhatta, life undergoes a change: 12–14 hours of work a day, loading and unloading bricks, compulsory sex with the owner or his men in the early hours of the night, sleep in the jhopdi in the late hours. No medical or sanitary arrangements.

A reja may have earned Rs 30–35 in a week, but receives only Rs 15 as khoraki. The rest she never gets. When the kiln closes down, the reja is given a sari and a railway ticket. The rest, she is told, has been adjusted against her khoraki and the dadan her parents received.

None of these facts can be verified easily as there is no wage or attendance register, no employment card. Women in the late stages of pregnancy work, because there is no maternity leave. Their lot is worse than that of those in the unorganized sector. A beggar can go abegging where he chooses. A contract labourer cannot. He does not have any freedom.

What drives them to the brick kilns? Poverty does. Poverty and the deep-rooted apathy of the state government towards adopting any remedial measures to remove the root causes of chronic poverty. Singbhum and Ranchi. The cradles of the Kal, Tamar, Birsa, Jharkhand and other movements. By the Bihar Government's own admission, Chhotanagpur has only two per cent land area under irrigation and five per cent under electrification. Only the industries and the towns receive electricity. There is no arrangement for irrigation through electricity. Lift irrigation is for show and publicity, not for the cultivator. The Chaibasa project is supposed to be under operation, but thousands of villages do not have even a well for drinking water. Under Gua police station, the tribals drink water from the Koina river which is polluted by the Khiriburu washery plant. The Munda-dominated Khunti subdivision has had no project for irrigation.

The Bihar Government collects, on each rupee paid towards land rent, 40 paise as cess for health, 40 paise as cess for education and 20 paise as cess for roads. Sounds very nice and reads better on paper. But how is this money spent in the region from where the contract-bound labourers come? Banka, under Chaibasa police station, has no school building, though there is a teacher. Guigaon under Chakradharpur police station has a school building. Dalbhanga is a predominantly Munda region and is now under Kuchai police station within Seraikela subdivision. It belonged to Tamar police station till 1954. Then came the Boundary Commission and, in order to have Oriya-majority Seraikela within Singbhum, Bihar, 30 moujas from the predominantly Mundari language area under Tamar police station were added to Seraikela. Seraikela became a part of Singbhum. But the Mundas of this region are not at all happy over the surgical operation on the regional map. They have to keep close connections with the Mundari area for social purposes and they feel cut off. In 1968 the government took over a high school at Dalbhanga and a hostel for the tribal students. Both were built with mud. The Bihar Government has not found time to convert these into pucca buildings in 13 years, nor funds to repair them. These are only a few of the innumerable instances of governmental apathy towards the tribal regions. There are lakhs and lakhs of tribals in Singbhum and Ranchi. A majority of them pay land rent. What does the almighty sarkar do with the 40 paise cess per rupee of land rent they pay for education?

For the poor tribal, money is blood. Land is tanr, banjhara. Each rupee is earned by selling so many bundles of firewood, so many baskets of chiranji, by breaking so many stones, by working so many hours in the mines. Even after the sanction of a primary school for every 100 homesteads, the people remain illiterate. In many schools the teachers don't attend work. They have their own business or trade or shop to look after.

The pradhan of Sagipi Primary School carries on a brisk business buying mowa, goats, silkworm, etc., from the villagers and selling them to traders. This worthy was once gheraoed. Complaints against him were submitted to the proper authority, but to no avail. Teachers from north Bihar posted in the tribal region have been caught lending money, buying land or taking bandobasti land. Stipends for Scheduled Caste and tribal boys in primary schools are a great blessing to the teachers who take a nice 'cut' from the money which is sent in lump sums. A Mundari song runs like this:

> Rando, Rando, come to school!
> Mata, Mata, where are you?
> Rando and Mata and the other boys
> Graze the cow, tend the goat.
> The Masterji sits in his shop.

The tribals pay 40 paise for health and medical care and what do they get in return? Lotapahar has a primary health unit but no doctor. So the unit is useless. Dulmi has a doctor but the health unit building is only half-built. Kukru has a dispensary attended by a compounder but no medicine and no doctor. Chhotonagra under Gua police station has no doctor but there is a dispensary. Situated in the deep interior, Chhotonagra did not have any Sahus till 1962. Now there are four Sahus who act as moneylenders, land-usurpers and police agents. The poor of the area are malaria-ridden. Women die at childbirth. Infant and child mortality is high.

The lack of doctors and medicine causes death. And when death, disease or epidemic frequents the lonely villages, the villagers launch a witch-hunt, identify someone as a witch and kill her. In Sagipi village in 1978 child mortality was high. The villagers were sure that a witch was causing these deaths. An old Christian tribal woman was identified as the witch. She was a person of some means, had a husband, grown-up sons, grandchildren. The villagers invited her for a diang (rice liquor) drinking session and killed her. In January 1981, at Dhangaon under Chakradharpur police station, a Ho woman aged 54 was killed in broad daylight. After a week her widowed daughter was also killed at night, while she was sleeping with her children in their hut. Reason? Some four or five people were suffering from the same sort of sore on their right legs. The witch must have caused those sores.

Chiriburu Mahila Samaj, under the leadership of the courageous woman, Laru Jonko, has launched a mass signature campaign against witch-hunting. Their cry is, 'Medical facilities are needed. This witch-hunting is barbarous and wrong. Doctors and medicine will bring succour to the people. We achieve nothing by killing innocent women.'

Till now almost Rs 3,000 crores have been spent on 'tribal development' in Chhotanagpur. The Sixth Plan has allotted Rs 800 crore. But even after five plans nothing has reached the area. The people have been left in primeval darkness. Officially, the leasing of forests to contractors has been abolished. The declaration has been given much publicity. The announcement came after the Gua firing. But contractors are felling trees in the Jaraikela forest under Sarenda division, all right. The forests in the Ranka mouja under Chandil police station are serving their death sentence. Mango, jamun, pial, fiendu, bael, all fruit-bearing trees, are exempt from felling under the Forest Acts. But the contractor's axe is felling them, too. The tribals and poor villagers are, naturally, desperate. After the Gua firing, the government declared that there would be no collection from the weekly haats. The haat masul (levy) was abolished. Yet haat masul is definitely exacted in one of the biggest haats of Singbhum district, the Kukru haat under Ichagarh police station. Previously, the masul was shared equally by the tribal buyer and the north Bihari seller. Now the purchaser of a cow or vegetables or paddy or clothes has to pay the full amount. In the dry months haat masul from Kukru is Rs 2,000 per week. In winter it is Rs 4,000. The Raja of Ichagarh is the recipient of this masul which is said to be collected for the development of Ichagarh High School. It is hard to understand why this school has not been taken over by the government. It is certain that the money does nothing for the school. Students pay their fees. The school goes on. The landless Jhora people have been running the ferry boats on the Koel, Koina and Subarnarekha for ages. Now the Bihar Government has leased out the ferries to contractors. The Jhoras are unemployed. At places the village panchayat has been handling the contracts.

What happens to the kendu or bidi leaves? Previously the poor villagers grew kendu trees on their land and sold the leaves to the traders. January to March is the plucking season. A family could earn Rs 400–500 per season. The Bihar Government leased out the plucking right to contractors; now the villagers are the contractors' labourers. For 100 kendu leaves (about a kg) he receives Rs 1.75 when he plucks in a government forest. And in the open market the rate is Rs 10 per kg. The contractors' rate is Re 1 for 100 keris or bundles. One keri contains 25 leaves. To pluck 2,500 leaves a man or a woman works from 4 in the morning till 4 in the afternoon in the depths of the forest, and receives

Re 1. The contractor will sell that quantity for Rs 250. I cite these figures to show the pattern of exploitation.

The Mahalis, like the Jhoras, have been reduced to destitution. They are traditionally basket-weavers. Previously they collected bamboo from the forests. Then came forest laws. They had to obtain permission from the Forest Department and pay masul for bamboo, the raw material for baskets and winnows. The ruthless deforestation by the contractors has caused them great suffering.

Tales of woe and exploitation on the one hand; the pulse of resistance mounting on the other. The Jharkhand demand is set against such a background. When these people take to violence, they do it out of sheer desperation.

I started with contract labourers and shall conclude my account with them. Not only women, men, too, are helpless. I cite two cases.

Amar Ekka, a Christian Munda and the son of Albis Ekka, was 19 years old in 1976. The family had eight members, 10 to 12 acres of land with a yield of 30 maunds. Amar was educated up to class 8. Fagu Sahu recruited him in 1976. Amar says, 'I went to Hurda Basar and this agent said that he would take us to Punjab and get us good jobs. I went to Bano, from there to Tati, from Tati to Batia, from Batia to Gomoh. At Gomoh I got into the Amritsar Mail. We got down at Tanda Hurmur station. Then we went along with Mahendra Singh who was the coolie agent for Punjab. Fagu Sahu sold us to Mahendra. We were five or six boys. We stayed for eight days at Pathankot. The farmer Makhan Singh promised to pay Rs 60 per month as wages plus food, clothes, etc. From 4 a.m. I looked after cattle till 8 a.m. From 8 a.m. I watered the wheat fields. I was ill-treated, beaten and harassed by Makhan Singh and his family members. My wage was raised to Rs 80. After six months I wanted to leave. Makhan did not give me two months' wages. He said he had paid me and was adjusting the money. I ran away from his place one day at 3 a.m. By train reached Tanda Hurmur. There Darshan Singh, a teacher, employed me at Rs 100 per month. He had 2,000 cows and buffaloes and milking was operated electrically. I worked till 1979 and my wage was Rs 175 per month. Then I left.'

Sura Pai, a Raotia boy from Buruichanda was brought to Ferozepur by Shivshankar Sahu and sold to Diwan Singh of Sandwala for Rs 250. 'Diwan Singh told me, "I have purchased you, so I won't give you anything for two months. After two months, I will pay you Rs 100 a month with food." I worked there for four months and was inhumanly treated. The local agricultural labourers asked me, "Why do you work for so little? We work for Rs 10–12 a day." I ran away after four months when my owner refused to pay me anything. I sold some wheat for Rs 8 and went by train to Ludhiana. There I met Barna Karkota of Harta village who was sold to Surjeet Singh, Diwan Singh's brother and a sarpanch. Barna was running away from his owner, a very cruel man. At Ludhiana we worked at Jagdamba Wool Mill at Rs 170 per month and four hours' overtime benefit. After two months I got Rs 180 per month. I spent Rs 100 on food and lodging. After I saved some money I returned home.'

We know some of these details from Purnendu Mazoomdar's untiring efforts to uncover the pattern of exploitation in Singbhum and Ranchi. The Bihar Government realizes Rs 30 crores from the forests of Chhotanagpur and Rs 10 crores from the excise department. The royalty received from the mines and industries must be fabulous. If forest revenue received by the government is Rs 30 crores, what must the contractors be earning? Their palaces in Ranchi and north Bihar give some idea. As long as Chhotanagpur is kept for exploitation alone, agents and sardars will go on haunting the destitute villages. Men and women will migrate to faraway places. Some will come back, some will not. Punjab and Haryana will have slaves. West Bengal and the rest of Bihar, bhatta-coolies. Kiln owners, mastaans and truck drivers will have their pound of flesh and all will be happy except the tribals and the non-tribal poor. But they are expendable.

Land Alienation among Tribals in West Bengal

Both in terms of law and their implementation, West Bengal has a relatively better record in land reforms than most other states of the country. The main comprehensive Land Reforms Act of the state was enacted in 1955 and has been amended several times since. In the main set of Acts and their subsequent amendments several provisions have been incorporated to prevent alienation of tribal land, particularly from tribals to non-tribals. But despite all these laws, the process of land alienation has reached serious proportions in the state.

It is true that there are several reasons for this, including the poor level of development among the tribals, lack of literacy and education among them,

---

Bortika, October–December 1989; and incorporating segments from 'Tribal Land Alienation', *Frontier*, 3 August 1991. Translated from the original Bengali by Maitreya Ghatak.

and their deep-rooted mistrust and fear of the legal system. But the real cause is their class position. India, that is, Bharat, doesn't consider them to be an integral part of society. How else can one explain the role played by the dominant sections of society, the administration and the political parties, doing everything within their means to ensure that the tribals do not enjoy any right to which they are entitled?

Under the laws of the state, a tribal can sell his land only to a tribal and any sale or even gift to a non-tribal is illegal. Sale or transfer of land to a non-tribal can be done only with the written permission of specially designated revenue officials. In case of a tribal seeking to transfer his land, the district and subdivision-level SC and ST Welfare Officers have been empowered to act as Revenue Officers and the formalities have to be carried out through them. Any violation of these provisions would make the transaction illegal.

A tribal can, however, transfer his land, without selling it, in a few specific cases:

— He can transfer the land to another tribal for a period not exceeding seven years under usufructuary mortgage (called khại khalasi in rural areas) against money borrowed. The idea is that the person who had lent the money would recover the loan with interest from the crops within the mortgage period. If, however, the loanee is in a position to repay the remaining amount before the stipulated period, the Revenue Officer would ensure that he regained his land on payment of the remaining amount.

— He can sell or gift the land to the government for a charitable purpose.

— He can mortgage the land to the government or to a registered cooperative society.

— No interest in land or transfer of the land itself by a tribal would be legal unless registered according to the provisions of the law.

— If any tribal had transferred any land to a non-tribal in contravention of the laws within a period of 30 years prior to the amendment of 1976, the transferred land would have to be restored to him.

The very idea behind specially empowering the SC and ST Welfare Officers to act as Revenue Officers (or kanungos) relating to transfer of tribal land was that they would have an advantage in protecting tribal interests by virtue of their official position. I learnt from the Land and Land Revenue Minister of West Bengal (no less!) that the necessary notification empowering these officials had been sent to them at the district and subdivision level after the amendments were made. It was sent once again after my enquiry. However, whenever a tribal approaches the SC and ST Officer at the district or subdivision level, he finds that either the concerned officials are not aware of the notification or they are evasive about it. The net result is that the tribals do not get the support of the Act. This is the general experience of a large number of tribals in Bankura, Medinipur, Darjeeling, Purulia, Hooghly and South 24

Parganas district. Due to their poverty, lack of education and the callousness and even collusion of officials with land sharks, land is constantly being transferred to non-tribals. I shall discuss two cases here. Both the cases have taken place in north Bengal, hardly a few kilometres away from Naxalbari.[1]

In the first case, some businessmen from outside the state are taking over the land of the local tribals at Ethelbari in Alipurduar subdivision of Jalpaiguri district. They are running a flourishing brick-making business. The pradhan (head of the village panchayat) is turning a blind eye to it. According to the villagers, he himself has an interest in the brick kilns. The upapradhan or the next person in the village panchayat, protested against this. The brick-kiln owners went to the police. The police promptly acted to protect the interests of the brick-kiln owners. On 20 August 1987, the Subdivisional Police Officer came to the village

---

1 Naxalbari, in far northern West Bengal, gave its name to the Naxalite movement after a tribal peasant uprising against local landlords in 1967.

with 60 policemen and beat up a large number of tribal men, women and even children. The upapradhan, himself a tribal, was not spared, because he had taken the side of the villagers against the brick-kiln owners.

The residents of Ethelbari have been trying to draw the attention of the authorities for the last few years, protesting against the brick kilns on their land. They had sent letters to the District Magistrate of Jalpaiguri, Subdivisional Land Reforms Officer, SC and ST Welfare Department, the Chief Minister, the Minister of Agriculture, the Superintendent of Police of the district and the Prime Minister of the country. No one cared to reply. Finally, an organization of tribals wrote a letter to the Supreme Court of the country. The Deputy Registrar of the Supreme Court wrote to the State Social Welfare Department, the Chairman of the Legal Aid Advisory Committee and to the Deputy Secretary of the Law Department of the state. There has been no response from any of them.

But how did the brick-kiln owners get access to the land they are occupying? In four out of a total of five cases, some money has been paid to the owners and then the land has been transferred to fictitious tribal people. It should be noted that this is the most widely prevalent method for registering sale of tribal land. Land is purchased in the name of people who do not exist, or do not have anything to do with the transaction other than lending their name. The person who actually buys the land is not a tribal but has money and political clout. It is not difficult for him to influence the local political parties, panchayat, police and officials—in other words, the very people who should protect the interests of the tribals. On how many fronts can the tribal carry on his battles?

In the fifth case, a non-tribal has declared himself to be a tribal and got the transaction registered.

These cases, if anything, expose the blatant violation of laws that goes on all the time. It is not enough to enact laws without making sure that they are also implemented. All these people continue to violate the laws with impunity.

A major problem is that the tribals do not even know that the SC and ST Welfare Officers are competent to provide them redress. The officials themselves seem to have no concern for a matter that is of such vital importance to the tribals. Restoration of illegally transferred land is possible only through the legal process, which is often protracted and always expensive. But the system that exists for providing legal aid to the poor people in this state is a farce. What generally happens is that whenever an aggrieved tribal goes to the police to make a complaint or seek protection, the police get the tribal implicated in false lawsuits. The lawyers of the government end up fighting against the tribal, instead of protecting him. Those who take over land from the tribals in total violation of laws can do so because they have the necessary clout and are helped not only by the police and the administration, but—and this is more serious—by the political parties of all colours and shades.

These political parties have destroyed the unity among the tribals and they usually operate through a small section of privileged tribals who do not protect the interests of the community and often create discord amongst fellow-tribals at the grassroots level.

After the 1982 elections, when the Left Front came to power for the second time, there was general jubilation among the landless and poor peasants and sharecroppers. There was widespread apprehension among the jotedars[2] and rich peasants that their surplus land would be taken over by the government. So far, many of them had been supporters of the Congress Party and most used to exploit the agricultural labourers, sharecroppers and marginal farmers. They sensed the winds of change and started switching sides. They mostly became supporters of the major partner in the Left Front, the Communist Party of India (Marxist).

---

2 Jotedars were substantial rural landholders or rich peasants in Bengal's agrarian order.

With these sections joining the ruling parties, those within the Left Front, particularly within the two Communist parties, who had been fighting for the poor peasants and sharecroppers, started feeling cornered inside their own parties. The very people against whom they had so far been fighting for land and for sharecroppers' rights, even achieving major success, were now within the ranks of their own parties. But their class interest remained unchanged. Now, as members of the major partner in the ruling Left Front, they had all the backing of the administration and there was little to prevent them from evicting sharecroppers even if they belonged to their own parties, or taking over the land of the small peasants. In several areas in West Bengal, tribal peasants and sharecroppers of the major ruling party had to fight against jotedars who belonged to their own party and community.

The other side of the picture is that if an ordinary peasant does not belong to the ruling parties, he does not have any protection. Take the case of Pasupati Murmu, a tribal peasant of Medinipur district. Pasupati belonged to the CPI, which was not a partner in the ruling Left Front in 1982. He had an acre of land for a family of nine. As this was not sufficient for survival, the members of his family used to work as agricultural labourers. But as he was outside the ruling parties, his land was forcibly taken over by the local panchayat and distributed among landless tribals. When he objected and tried to harvest paddy from his own land, he was mercilessly beaten up and killed and his family forced to leave the village. I had repeatedly informed the district administration of Medinipur and the Land and Land Reforms Department of the state about the incident, seeking restoration of the land to his family. Nothing happened.

The reason why I am mentioning this incident is that party politics has sown seeds of bitter conflict and violence at the grassroots level among the tribals. All the political parties are doing this, directly or indirectly, and causing division among the tribals, all for narrow party interests. This has further complicated the issue of land alienation among tribals and those eyeing the land take advantage of this.

These crafty people are fully aware that even the educated among the tribals do not know of the laws which could help them get back land already transferred, or that officers at the district and subdivision level have been empowered to help them. They know that the tribals are unaware of the benefits of the 1986 amendments to the laws relating to restoration of transferred land.[3] This ignorance is fairly widespread. I have received a large number of applications and documents from tribals who have lost their land in the districts of South 24 Parganas, Bankura and Purulia, which proves how pervasive this ignorance is.

Those who take advantage of this also know that the tribal would get no help from the local officials and the police, as no one would listen to him. Any tribal without clout would ultimately

---

3 The 1986 amendment inserted section 14HH, concerning the setting aside of sales of land belonging to Scheduled Tribe raiyats in execution of decrees.

have to abandon his rights and hand over the land to the land sharks because they have money and influence. Those showing the audacity to seek legal redress would get lost in the labyrinth of unending civil suits.

They also know that if the tribal goes to the panchayat or political parties, he would not get any justice, as these are controlled by the mainstream people. The simple tribal, not used to lying or the complex ways of the legal system, loses his case even before he starts it. As a result:

— Land is often bought in the name of a non-existent tribal or a tribal who acts as a front for a non-tribal buyer. The concerned departments oblige by registering the sale-deed, once a few palms are greased. No inconvenient queries are made, of course.

— In more blatant cases, a non-tribal manages to procure (read buy) a certificate identifying himself as a tribal, and through further fraudulent means gets the land transferred in his own name without the knowledge of the actual tribal owner.

Other means are simpler but no less effective. The Ethelbari case gives some idea of this—through political clout and with help from obliging panchayats, the police and goons, if necessary, the lawful tribal owners are physically evicted from their own land. When goons terrorize people, they are supposed to go to the police. But if the police are hand-in-glove with them, what chance do the people have? It is not the tribals alone who are at the receiving end of this process. But this is certainly happening more in the case of tribals.

One aggravating factor in the case of a tribal is that he often does not keep papers and documents properly. If he is told that all the papers should be carefully preserved, he is nonplussed and wonders why, since everyone knows that he owns a particular piece of land, he needs papers to prove it. It may sound amazing, but I have met such people. They just do not understand many of our ways, the ways of mainstream society.

Those among them who understand the importance of papers and documents face numerous problems in trying to get the documents or their copies from concerned offices. In this matter, the worst culprits are the Land Revenue Department personnel.

While papers are necessary, they may not be enough, as Agnu Panna learnt the hard way. Agnu is an Oraon. His forefathers, along with thousands of other indentured tribal labourers, were brought from Bihar and Madhya Pradesh to the tea-garden area in north Bengal over a hundred years ago.[4] The tribals were brought to several other areas of West Bengal to clear forests and reclaim land for agriculture.

Agnu's forefathers were brought to the Matigara police station area in the Siliguri subdivision. If it doesn't ring a bell, the place is within walking distance of a place called Naxalbari, a name that has become a symbol of

---

4 North Bengal tea plantations drew heavily on nineteenth-century indentured labour from Scheduled Tribe communities of the Chotanagpur plateau.

the protest and struggle of peasants and oppressed people all over the country. But that was of little help to Agnu Panna.

Agnu's father was a regular tenant of 32.99 acres of land since pre-Independence days and he used to pay annual rent and had all the papers and documents in order. When zamindari was abolished after the passing of the Estate Acquisition Bill in 1954, it was suddenly discovered that Agnu's father's name was no longer in the records and the land was shown to be in the name of Shiva, the family deity of the landlords under whom his father was a tenant. This was nothing unusual, as records of debates in the West Bengal Legislative Assembly would show—crafty landlords even recorded their lands in the names of animals. Transfer of land in the name of a family deity was very much within the purview of the law. Only, in this specific case, he who got the land transferred in his family deity's name did not have a right to the land. But such small problems are easily surmountable for people with money and influence.

This blatant manipulation of records could only have been possible in connivance with the land revenue officials. When Agnu's father went to his own land, he was severely beaten up by the landlord's goons.

Agnu's father complained to the Land Revenue Department office at Siliguri and an order was issued in his favour, nullifying the earlier change. Agnu was a minor at that time. Then the landlord submitted a forged document and got the land recorded in the name of his own brother-in-law. Then the same land was transferred by the brother-in-law to the son of the landlord. Thus, the same piece of land was transferred twice, all on the basis of forged documents, in total violation of section 5(A) of the relevant law. This, too, could only have been possible with the cooperation of the Land Revenue Department officials.

Then a part of the land thus acquired was sold off by the landlords and the deal was duly registered. After several years, the landlord Kaliprasad died. By that time, Agnu had joined the Border Security Force (BSF) and was serving in its 93rd Regiment in Nagaland and Tripura. The son of the landlord brought an eviction suit against Agnu's father and his family, from their own land. This was also a blatantly false case and ultimately the judgement went in favour of Agnu's family.

The son of the landlord started a new lawsuit against Agnu's family, claiming their land. The case was started in 1979 and dragged on for years. All this time Agnu, who was posted away from Siliguri, had to make arrangements for following up the cases. While the case was dragging on, the landlord's son sold off the land to some local criminal elements, generally described in West Bengal as 'antisocials'. By the time the case ran its full course and the order went in favour of Agnu and his family, the antisocials had already forcibly evicted them from their land and built a house there. Agnu had to take leave several times to follow up the case. He needed more leave now. But the BSF sacked him without showing any reason, after many years of service.

Throughout this period, when these blatant violations of law were taking place, Agnu and his father complained to the police station. Records show that between 1976 and 1987, 24 formal complaints were made at the Siliguri and Matigara police stations. Of them six were made in 1976, three in 1977, two in 1978, three in 1979, two in 1980, one in 1982, two in 1986 and five in 1987. But this tribal family didn't have a chance against the machinations of the landlord, antisocials and the police working together.

During this period, Agnu's family sent applications to a large number of people, praying for intervention and justice. The list includes the District Judge; Deputy Commissioner; Superintendent of Police; SC and ST Welfare Department, Darjeeling district; Subdivisional Officer; Subdivisional Police Officer and Scheduled Tribe Welfare Officer of Siliguri subdivision; the local head of the panchayat; Settlement Officer, Cooch Bihar; the Chief Minister and Land Reforms Minister, West Bengal; the Law Minister; the Home Minister; and the Prime Minister of India and many others. To no avail, of course.

Though the State Land Revenue Minister has repeatedly declared that tribal land cannot be acquired and converted into tea gardens, this is happening nevertheless. One example of this is the Nagpur tea garden which is being developed over 450 acres near Belakoba, adjacent to Siliguri in north Bengal. The land has been mainly acquired from the tribals.

Fatinga and Paglidhuri villages are under Sikarpur mouja. Nagpur tea-garden owners have acquired most of the land of these two villages. As a result, 61 tribal families of Fatinga and 101 from Paglidhuri have been rendered landless. Except for one family, the rest are tribals. The Nagpur tea-garden owners have acquired about 477 acres of land from them. The acquirement process was started in June 1989 by middlemen. The land was surveyed in December 1989. It is learnt that each family was paid at the rate of Rs 1,000 per acre. Ninety per cent of the acquired land of Paglidhuri is patta land.[5] The Fatinga tribals, too, had patta land.

5 Patta land is land held under a patta, or written title/settlement document.

In acquiring tribal land, Nagpur tea-garden owners allegedly resorted to foolproof methods. It appears that 162 tribal families of the two villages are applying to the tea-garden owners and giving them land voluntarily. This appeal is written on a Rs 20 stamp paper. It reads like this: 'On 23.12.89, we have given to you land owned by us, till date cultivated by us, sustaining our livelihood. You, too, have helped us by giving Rs 1,000 per acre. You will give the land-giving families one job per acre . . .' It ends like this: 'We will enjoy the same facilities and benefits followed by other tea gardens, such as schools, permanent jobs as labourers, rations, bonus, hut, fuels, hospitals, clubs, work-tools, umbrellas, blankets, etc. Whatever we have written here is just a repetition of your promises.'

The Divisional Commissioner, Jalpaiguri, said that administrative letters were issued to all new tea-garden owners to postpone work. It is clear that this letter did not deter the Nagpur tea-garden owners from proceeding with plantation work.

The cases discussed here are merely examples of what goes on in the state, under all regimes.

Numerous other similar incidents are taking place all the time. I receive complaints from tribals over loss of land almost every week. And this happens despite the existence of laws for the protection of the tribals with specific responsibility given to the administration and the police. Unfortunately, those contributing most to the process of land alienation among tribals are the officials and the police themselves. It is through their direct support that the process goes on. Political parties who could have ensured the proper implementation of the laws in favour of the tribals remain silent spectators, or even worse. In none of the districts of West Bengal have they taken up this issue. It is also a harsh reality that people belonging to the various political parties are themselves involved in depriving the tribals of their land.

With a mainstream society long used to exploiting them, a bureaucracy that is, at best, indifferent to their problems, and political parties mainly interested in mobilizing their votes, the largely illiterate and numerically few tribals can do little. In recent years, after every election, many tribals have been branded as 'non-supporters' of the ruling front and thus turned into vulnerable prey for land sharks. The influx of immigrants first from East Pakistan and then from Bangladesh, further complicated matters. In the neighbouring state of Tripura, it has entirely changed the demographic composition, reducing the tribals to a minority in a few years.[6] In the northern parts of West Bengal, also, the periodic influxes accentuated the process of land transfer from the tribals.

And now, with the recent changes in economic policy and the obsession with big projects, the process is likely to be accentuated. Already, in the erstwhile West Dinajpur district of north Bengal, large-scale conversion of agricultural land into tea estates has started. Another factor that has contributed to the eviction of tribals from the Terai region of north Bengal is the repressive action of the police in the

---

6 Tripura's tribal majority was transformed after Partition and migration from East Pakistan.

name of containing the Gorkhaland movement.[7] A large number of tribals have already been evicted from this area. With the prospect of the movement taking a new course, that of demanding a separate state, this process may be further accentuated.

In West Bengal, the Santhals are numerically and otherwise stronger than the other tribal groups. But even they are often forced to part with their land in the face of the combined assault of political parties–bureaucracy–rural rich–brick-kiln owners–antisocials–panchayats–development projects. The panchayats have become the den of vested interests in rural areas.

The least that the government can do is to inform the tribals about the laws which exist for protecting their rights to land. The legal provisions should be explained in simple language and widely circulated among the tribals. They should be displayed in panchayat

7 The Gorkhaland movement was the demand, centered on Darjeeling and surrounding hill, Terai and Dooars areas, for a separate state for Indian Gorkhas; its major 1986–88 phase was followed by the creation of the Darjeeling Gorkha Hill Council.

offices at all levels. Repeated announcements should be made over the radio and TV. Why are they not being published in the Bengali and Santhali publications of the state government, titled West Bengal, and the very largely circulated daily newspaper of the CPI(M)?

The government needs to send circulars to the district and subdivision-level SC and ST Welfare Officers on a regular basis, informing them of their legal obligations. Special courts should be formed in areas with a high tribal concentration.

Another important step that needs to be taken is the formation of legal aid cells for the tribals, which won't exploit the tribals and will take up their cases as public interest litigations. While a lot of initiative has to be taken by the tribals themselves, they alone cannot go far without support from the more aware and responsible sections of the mainstream. A beginning has to be made, and made now. Or else, by the time the country reaches the 21st century, most of the tribals who have land today will be landless. If that happens, the smaller tribal groups would be completely wiped off the map of the country.

Eucalyptus: Why?

'Eucalyptus is a myrtaceous genus of trees, mostly Australian. Most of them secrete resinous gums, whence they are called gum trees' (Webster's Dictionary). Stebbing's *The Forests of India* (1926) has only a few words for eucalyptus. The genus is also referred to as an experiment in new plantation.

In the 1961 District Gazetteer of Palamau and Singbhum, in the chapters on forests, there is not a single reference to eucalyptus. Nor in a handbook prepared and published by the Government of West Bengal does one come across the name now deified by union and state governments. The destruction of natural forests and the plantation of eucalyptus is quite a recent

---

Economic and Political Weekly, 6 August 1983.

affair. The eucalyptus policy and the insane and ruthless new forest bill are closely linked.[1]

Forests consist of trees, plants, creepers, shrubs, bushes and undergrowth of grass and lesser plants. A lot has been written about sal forests but almost all Indian trees have a social and economic relevance to the immediate society. In the Bouddha Jatakas we come across a story—Jeevaka, Gautama Buddha's physician, was once sent to a forest by his teacher to collect plants that have no use for mankind. Jeevaka came back after a long search and said that he had failed to find any such plant. In the book *Common Trees* published by the National Book Trust, H. Santapau has discussed 36 trees and plants. Kadam, 'in Bombay forests, is considered after teak, one of the five most valuable timber trees'. It has medicinal properties as well. The

1 The reference is to the proposed Indian Forest Bill of 1980, which met broad opposition from forest-rights and environmental groups and was not enacted. The separate Forest (Conservation) Act, 1980 came into force retrospectively from 25 October 1980 and restricted the dereservation or non-forest use of forest land without central approval.

flame of the forest or the palash serves mankind with lac, gum, seed, leaf and firewood, and due to its adaptability to dry, sandy and hilly areas is a good species for the regeneration of poor soil. The mowa has so many economic uses that in the proposed Jharkhand area of West Bengal it is justifiably known as Kalpataru or the divine tree.[2] Lodha brides are first married to the mowa tree, then to the groom, who has to get married first to a mango tree. Toon, bhendi, tamarind, kusum, jackfruit, ironwood, gliricide, amaltas, purple bauhinis, silk cotton, kendu, mussaenda, the tree of heaven, all have economic uses and a mixed forest sustains the immediate populace. Not all of them are tribals. In the forest areas, tribals and non-tribals, all the poor people, somehow make a living from the forest. We, in India, know very little about the economic uses of our trees. We know about the traditional uses only. Any advanced country (other than India) in 36 years, would have undertaken extensive research on the

---

2 The Jharkhand movement historically referred to a wider Adivasi political-cultural region extending beyond the boundaries of the state later created from southern Bihar in 2000.

subject and, with a sensible forest policy, would have made maximum use of the knowledge.

Take the case of Jhargram and Purulia of West Bengal. A carefully grown forest of sal, palash, kendu, piasal, wild jamun, jackfruit, amla, plum and other species would have provided the region with food, fuel and various means of livelihood. Such a forest would help life to flourish and, importantly, the soil moisture would be retained. Only such a forest justifies the term 'social forestry' because it sustains the neighbouring rural society.

And, from the not-so-old District Gazetteers of Bihar, we find that the government's forest policy was not always aimed at the total destruction of natural species. The 1961 Gazetteer on Singbhum states that sal was the principal forest product of that district. Only a small quantity of simul and other softwood species were supplied to Western India Match Company. The Palamau Gazetteer stated that sal sometimes constituted 50 per cent of the crop and stressed the importance of bamboo cultivation, as it was in great demand at the paper mills. There is not a single reference to eucalyptus in the Gazetteers of the two districts mainly dependent upon forest revenue. Today, with finance from Sweden, Singbhum is felling natural forests and planting eucalyptus. WIMCO needs eucalyptus for the matchbox industry. I was shocked to see Palamau robbed of the magnificent bamboos, palash, kusum, sidha, shisham and sal, and newly clothed in eucalyptus. But it is still possible to come across real forests in Palamau and Singbhum here and there. In the Bankura, Purulia and Medinipur districts of West Bengal, it is all eucalyptus. Our villagers have been robbed of food, fuel and means of survival because of the state's social forestry policy.[3] One cannot eat the leaf, bark or fruit of eucalyptus. Eucalyptus does not offer shelter from sun and rain. But protest against

3 Social forestry in India was promoted in the late 1970s and 1980s as a response to fuelwood scarcity and rural development needs; eucalyptus was widely used because it grew rapidly and supplied poles, pulpwood and fuel, but it also became a focus of protest where plantations displaced local subsistence uses.

eucalyptus, in West Bengal, is interpreted as the influence of Jharkhandi propaganda.

Why this sudden forest-departmental frenzy for eucalyptus? Well, eucalyptus means matchboxes, rayon, furniture, medicine. Which class benefits from factories, workshops, plants and markets connected with various eucalyptus products? Definitely not the poor and the downtrodden. The forest is meant for society and society is sustained by the forest. I have not heard of a Ho from Singbhum, or a Parhayiya from Palamau or a Lodha or Santhal from West Bengal who has gone in for big capital investment in eucalyptus products. Social forestry for which society? Not for the poor and the downtrodden. For the rich, then? It must be so. But at what national cost?

Eucalyptus was introduced to India in the 1840s from Australia. It could be seen in the big gardens of the well-to-do as a decorative tree. No country in the world really went in for eucalyptus plantation as it was not a safe tree to play with. As a full-grown eucalyptus consumes 80 gallons of water a day, it is not good for dry soil but beneficial for marshy land, and for the desert, where the sandy layer has already been exposed.[4] A sturdy species, eucalyptus will grow in any type of soil. The chief of Terai forests, Nainital division, admitted in 1975 that wherever eucalyptus plantations came up, the tubewells went dry and water levels of the wells fell. He had also noted that the forest floor in a eucalyptus plantation was devoid of undergrowth. According to experts, eucalyptus trees were to be uprooted if the river or stream nearby went dry.

According to ecologists of Bombay, the eucalyptus hazard was affecting the ecological balance of the Terai, where natural forests had been felled to make way for the eucalyptus. During the summer, the hot winds blowing from the plains got no resistance from the eucalyptus,

4 Later studies and policy debates have made the fixed '80 gallons' claim too blunt: eucalyptus water use varies by species, age, density, site and comparison crop. The broader controversy has persisted because plantation choices also affect soil, biodiversity, local employment and control over common lands. Rohit Pandit, 'Why Eucalyptus?', *Down to Earth*, 23 April 2018.

and hit the snowlines. Previously they would absorb the moisture of the Terais. As a result the Pindari glacier is already receding. Nainital and Mussoorie are not so cold anymore. In 1982, a world-renowned specialist on the subject had visited the Dehradun Forest Research Institute and expressed his dismay at seeing eucalyptus plantations between Dehradun and Rishikesh. He said that it was senseless to fell fruit and fuel-yielding trees to plant eucalyptus. Eucalyptus would suck the soil dry. If any tree in India needed uprooting, it was eucalyptus.

When I was touring the faraway regions of Purulia, a soil conservationist confided that the extensive eucalyptus plantations were consuming whatever little water the Purulia soil had. That no undergrowth covers a eucalyptus plantation floor is very apparent. Nature's process of creation also gets hampered, as the strong smell of eucalyptus repels flying insects like bees, butterflies, etc., causing pollination stoppage. A eucalyptus forest does not encourage or harbour wildlife of small animals and birds. I am concerned with the India I know. My India is of the poor, starving and helpless people.

Most of them are landless and the few who have land are happy to be able to make the most of given resources. To cover Purulia, Bankura, Medinipur, Singbhum and Palamau with eucalyptus will rob my India of drinking and irrigation water. These are the areas where there is a chronic water scarcity.

The water consumption of a eucalyptus tree is equal to that of 10 sal trees. Its slim trunk and narrow leaves are incapable of resisting wind. Nor can it offer shade. So the upper level of soil, which conserves water and nitrogen salt, gets eroded due to direct exposure to the sun and wind. The sandy sub-level gets exposed. During the monsoons this sand gets carried down to the river beds. Thus the rivers and streams of the dry areas are getting filled with sand, and denudation of vegetation on the banks is causing the widening of the river bed. Such rivers flood easily, causing havoc to the countryside.

It is downright hypocrisy to destroy the natural habitat of wildlife, to plant eucalyptus and yet to publicize India's great concern for the protection of wildlife.

An impartial and objective survey by a team of experts will prove that:

a) eucalyptus plantation is a threat to India's store of subsoil water reserve which is already diminishing;

b) it is a threat to the country's ecological and atmospheric balance;

c) eucalyptus plantation on the Himalayan foothills should be cut down and uprooted to protect the snowlines from the hot winds blowing from the plains;

d) rivers, streams, wells, tanks and tubewells in the eucalyptus area are drying up; and

e) it is monstrous to plant eucalyptus in the drought-prone regions of West Bengal, Bihar and elsewhere in India.

Such a team should also bring out who the beneficiaries from eucalyptus are and who the losers. Will eucalyptus sustain India's starving millions? How? Most of the bonded labourers of Palamau do not have rights over homestead land, though Bihar passed the land reform bill in 1952. The Kheria-Shabars of West Bengal are constantly being hounded by the forest guards and the police and regularly evicted from homesteads. The Lodhas of Medinipur lead a threatened existence. The Santhals of West Bengal are constantly on the move in search of work. The Birhors and Parhayiyas live like paupers in West Bengal and Bihar. In my India, children of seven years are hired out as child labourers just for a meal. Will eucalyptus help them? Are these people going to operate rayon, plastic or matchbox industries? Will they own and operate paper mills, or open furniture shops? We know the answer. Then for whom are we sacrificing our Himalayas, our monsoons, our agricultural fields, our people?

An anti-eucalyptus movement on a national scale seems to be the only answer. Since the eucalyptus-oriented forest policy and the abominable forest bill are closely linked together, such a movement should thwart and ultimately defeat both.

Witch-Hunting in West Bengal: In Whose Interest?

Superstitious belief is a terrible age-old malady. It exists in the dark lives of the deprived tribals of Purulia, Maldah and elsewhere. It has survived in other societies as well. The present-day urban people, including the frequently Europe-travelled rich, the middle class, the lower middle class, the poor—all are increasingly falling prey to antiquated beliefs in fortune-telling and the supernatural. In the last decade and a half, people have sought out novel gods and demons, religious gurus, astrologers and clairvoyants. The daily newspapers regularly publish what the stars foretell—this leads to a dependence on astrology and destiny instead of confidence in one's own abilities. Indian godmen, soothsayers and tantra

---

Bortika, June 1987. Translated from Bengali by Nabarun Bhattacharya.

plus all sorts of hocus-pocus, are flourishing in the US and Europe.

Perhaps the residents of cities like Calcutta read stories about witch-baiting among the tribals and think how hopelessly ignorant and superstitious these people are. On the other hand, many people in Europe and the US do think that India is the land of gods, yogis, hermits and the supernatural! In India, politicians run after astrologers. What I see clearly is that the belief in the supernatural has turned into a big business in the circles of the wealthy and the educated. When the privileged sections of the country become obsessed with superstition and the supernatural, and obscurantistic ideas spread unbridled among the deprived sections of the country, it seems that something unholy is behind the apparent. Could it be that there are interested quarters who want this country to remain immersed in the depths of darkness?

A highly educated couple has lost their only son—the boy contracted tetanus. Instead of giving him urgent medical help, the parents, residents of a city high-rise, were waiting for the divine ash of grace to fall from the framed photograph of a godman. A wife in a similar family had died from smallpox. They were rich and highly educated. They did not believe in vaccines since they were brahmans. They diligently worshipped their gods and did not belong to the so-called lower castes. Many such examples could be given. The other day I came across a book stating that witch circles have, of late, become very popular among Europeans, especially women. According to a very largely circulated Bengali newspaper, one Mr Premcharan Roy came to Jalpaiguri from Bangladesh to have his wife treated, and stayed with one Kulin Roy. Premcharan was lynched in the same house on being suspected as a 'witch'. Certainly the deceased did not belong to the tribals.

Faith in witch cults used to exist in tribal society. Suddenly it seems to have acquired a shot in the arm. I have my own explanation about their strong faith in witch cults. The tribals are losing whatever they had due to overwhelming socio-economic changes and all-devouring political pressures, over which they have little control. They are the hapless prey whom the wily hunters have been after for a long, long time. They are losing their land. They are deprived of education and are forced to work as migrant workers. Their culture is threatened by the vulgar onslaught of Jatra, films and video parlours. The political process has created an exploitative class within them, who flex their muscles as mafia dons. Ancient social mores are being eroded. The dowry system, earlier non-existent, has entered tribal life. Their languages are denied recognition. In numerous written histories of India, there is no reference to the countless tribal uprisings against the British imperialists. Neither the centre nor the state gives any award for tribal language and literature. They have been kept as museum pieces. In such a dismal scenario, it is natural for them to think that the witch cult is something which truly belongs to them, something of their own. Why should they have to lose everything? That is why they have embraced the cult with a new vigour, to preserve their identity.

This explanation is entirely mine. At the same time I know it's very easy to arouse the tribals by saying that something is 'purely a tribal matter'. Then one can see that it's not merely a matter of superstition. It's something entirely different. At the very sound of the term 'witch', the tribals forget all political differences and act in a frenzy, even victimizing one of their own.

The money collected through fines or from the land of those declared witches, is not spent to benefit the person whose disease or death triggered off the search for the 'witch'. A part of it is pocketed by the janguru, the person who actually identifies someone as a witch, and the rest goes on liquor and meat.

Laru Jonko, a tribal woman activist of Singbhum, sent me a shortlist in 1982. The list showed that 37 persons had been killed among the Ho tribals on suspicion of being witches, within a short span of time, most of them women. In each case, the design was to grab the land of the lynched. Laru also wrote that in order to stop witch killing, health centres should be established, medical treatment arranged to tackle infant mortality and diseases and a propaganda offensive launched to drive home the message that it is disease and not witchcraft that is responsible for death. After each and every killing, the concerned police stations were informed in Singbhum. But the police simply refused to come.

In this connection, the role of the police needs attention. In the books *Witch Killing among Santhals* and *Santhal Samaje Daini O Bartaman Sanskriti* (The Witch and Contemporary Culture in Santhal Society) by A. B. Chaudhuri, an officer of the West Bengal Police Department who has wide experience in the subject, it is clear that in the district of Maldah alone, during the period 1951–79, altogether 96 witch killings took place. Almost in every case, the police were informed and they took the necessary steps. During 1976–81, timely police interventions prevented 56 such killings.

Here I would like to draw the attention of the reader to the role of the police. Those who organized the anti-witch cult movement in Purulia in 1983–84, had to flee from their villages because of the wrath of zealots and political parties. The prompt setting up of police pickets helped them to return to their villages. The books by A. B. Chaudhuri inform us that whenever the police received information, action followed without fail. The administration had taken measures against witch enthusiasts in Islampur of West Dinajpur, and it worked. Once I wrote on the problem in a popular Bengali journal. After reading my article, a police officer, Prasanta Kumar Aich, wrote to me from West Dinajpur, a district in north Bengal. This letter, from a person who deals with the problem at the grassroots level, is quite revealing:

> I work in the West Bengal Police. From 1983–85, I worked as a sub-inspector in the Kanki check-post under Chakulia Police Station in the Islampore subdivision of West Dinajpur. In

1981 I was the Officer-in-Charge of this police station. During this period I kept a keen watch on the problems and troubles affecting the Santhal society. Because of this I, in my personal capacity, used to be in touch with the tribal quarters of Islampur and sought their cooperation in the solution of their various problems. I came across your article entitled 'Tribal Society and Witch Cult' in the journal *Paribartan* and liked it. But what saddens me is that there is no reference to the role of the police in this matter. In your article, you have mentioned the incident of Sundar Tudu. Through Mohan Hansda, I came to know about the incident, while I was posted at Kanki. The victim sought my protection. I summoned the people who had branded him a witch. I also asked Mohan Hansda to protect the family of the victim from assaults. I also sent a radio message to the SDO and requested him to send an officer of the tribal department. In front of the officer and invited Santhal leaders, I explained everything and solved the problem. The restive Santhals gave me a written assurance that they would not create any trouble whatsoever. I do not seek any compliments but do feel that the incident would inspire my colleagues in the police, if publicized.

After joining the Kanki Police Post I studied the typical problems of the tribal areas which lead to trouble and decided on a strategy. Accordingly, I trained a Santhal home guard and I used to ask Mohan Hansda and other Santhal leaders to come to the police post and solve problems amicably through discussions. Frequently I sought the assistance of officers from the tribal department. With the help of the above-mentioned well-meaning Santhals, I effectively neutralized the battle-cry of 'Bitlaha' which was raised in Jangatuli village by the Santhals. Otherwise many lives would have been lost. My experience shows that in most cases, witch killing could be prevented by adopting early measures, including meetings and discussions, which should be done, of course, with a certain tact. In the same way, the problem of the Bongaon witch case was amicably solved by the police in 1985. This year, the Hasan village witch case was also tackled similarly. In fact, a large number of cases have been tackled this way in the recent past. In each and every case, we invariably get the assistance of Pargana Mohan Hansda.

Behind these incidents are the religious beliefs of the Santhals, as well as personal enmity and disputes. I hold the same view as you that lack of education and scientific

> awareness, dearth of education among women, absence of adequate health facilities—all these are major causes. In conclusion I would like to add that a very good understanding and rapport exists between the tribal department and the police administration.

In the above cases, the role of the police is praiseworthy and I shall discuss this later. In fact, administrative initiatives in this regard started long ago. It becomes clear from the accounts of various tribal authors who have written in *Bortika* and elsewhere, that a few of them believe that witches are born with supernatural capabilities. Some others believe that they are specially initiated and not born with supernatural powers. There are specific norms and ritual hymns for the witches. Usually childless women, widows, older women or those with exceptionally ugly faces were considered witches in the Chhotanagpur division. Jangurus or shamans, known as Sokha, Mati, Deonra or Bhagat, used to find out the witches, who had to admit their guilt before panchayats and pay fines. Refusal to do so would lead to punitive beating, confiscation of land and, occasionally, expulsion from the villages.

Witches had their own tradition, with attendant norms. Similarly, witch-hunting also had its tradition, rules, trials and punishments. These were part of the social structure. We find in the *Palamau District Gazetteer* (1961) that the authorities are fully aware about its influence, especially about the witch-hunting Sokhas, but they are not doing anything to declare it illegal. It says that the Sokhas in the past had received the patronage of lower-level government staff, specially the police. It recommends that:

1. In schools in tribal areas and hostels for tribal students, teachers should take special care to explain to the students the real causes of illness and diseases. The teachers should also inform the students that in the developed areas of the country, belief in witches does not exist.

2. If any person is assaulted on suspicion of being a witch, then the assaulter should be punished legally.

3. The tribals blame the witches for their diseases. This attitude could be changed by making modern medical facilities available to the tribals.

We know that these have not been translated into reality. The virtues of electric light vis-à-vis the glow of the kerosene lamp can only be trumpeted if electricity is amply available. What is the use of tall claims in support of electricity where only fireflies light up dark dungeons? People will continue to believe in witches where modern medical facilities are not available. Moreover, we should keep in mind that the belief is nurtured by strong vested interests.

Reverend P. O. Bodding has an explanation for faith in witchcraft in his 'On Taboo and Customs Connected Therewith amongst the Santals' (1898).[5] According to him, the Santhal religion is mainly centred on the male. The women can only reach the gods through the men. They are debarred from approaching the

5 P. O. Bodding, 'On Taboo and Customs Connected Therewith amongst the Santals', *Journal of the Asiatic Society of Bengal*, 3 (1898): 1–24.

gods directly. The Santhal man and woman do not have mutual trust in their relationship. This is even true in their day-to-day lives. This leads the woman, for good or bad, to crave supernatural powers. They cannot do it openly, since the males do not approve. That is why they secretly study the witch cult. Bodding goes on to state that the shamans are criminals to the core. They have their sleuths who smell out information and may proclaim anyone as a witch. Often they are lynched to death. Previously they were dishonoured and hounded out.

When the administration turned a blind eye, personal initiatives were undertaken to stop witch killing. Bodding has narrated the exploits of one Assistant Commissioner of the Santhal Parganas who used a galvanic battery in a case where a woman had been branded a witch. When the woman touched the battery, the connecting wire was kept disconnected and she was spared a shock. But the witch-hunters suffered shocks and finally admitted their guilt.

Wilkinson said about Singbhum in 1838 that, 'Education should spread to fight the witch cult and Sokha practice. It is the Sokhas who make the occult calculations and detect the witch which leads to the death of the cursed woman. These practices have not stopped and lead to numerous killings annually.' Even towards the end of the 19th century, some writers had noticed that the jangurus had become mercenary and persons with vested interests had taken over the cult and led to its misuse. Dalton, the Commissioner of Singbhum, took measures to stop the Sokha system in 1860. He wanted both the Sokha and the person seeking his services to be proclaimed legal offenders.

Numerous incidents could be cited showing that those branded 'witches' or 'possessed' accept the charge and abide by the social pressures. Even in non-tribal societies, if someone is reared up on the belief that the 'possessed' will flee from a bed strewn with the leaves of a particular fruit, she is bound to get a shock on finding such a leaf on the bed because of the power of autosuggestion. Such a person would inevitably be declared 'possessed'.

In Dalton's *Ethnology of Bengal* (1872), we come across an incident when a Sokha accuses an elderly Ho woman of eating up someone's cow. The accused admitted that the cow had died because of her occult powers. This also proved, in turn, her occult prowess! The owner of the cow forgave her crime, but warned her that further evil offences would not be tolerated. Afterwards, the cow-owner's son died. The Sokha, as usual, blamed the old woman. She said that apart from her, three other women were also guilty of the crime. The dead son's father beheaded the four women, who did not try to escape. The father went to the police station on his own and confessed to everything during the trial.

Witch and Sokha, both are intractable truths. If this belief continues through generations, the inevitable is bound to happen. An ancient tradition has transmuted into a changed form. My information about Islampur shows that the agents of the jangurus keep track of local feuds, the landholdings of those involved, and secretly instigate one against the other. When the case reaches the janguru, he at once asks for a hefty sum of money. These jangurus are neither wise nor equal to the medicine men of ancient times. They are nothing but mercenaries. Those branded witches are also not the occult-loving women of yore—they are victims of feuds, political vendetta, clan hatred, greed and conspiracies. The sad fact is that previously the tribal could cope with disease and natural vagaries, with the help of his indigenous knowledge. His world was comprehensible to him. All that has gone. With his arsenal of ancient herbal medicines, he cannot fight the onslaught of numerous diseases, as the medicinal herbs have vanished together with the receding forests. Nor does he have access to modern medicine. He does not know that various mysteries can be explained by science and reason. In such a situation it is natural for him to seek the aid of the janguru.

I remember certain incidents. A Muslim bus driver of Maharashtra ran over a python and killed it. His children, since birth, had skin covered with scales like that of a snake. People called it the curse of the dead python and the children were ostracized. But a doctor diagnosed this as an incurable skin disease which is a result of frequent inter-marriage within the family. The disease, identified in 1881, still has no known cause. A girl in southern India had a nest of flying insects in her ears, but the reason is unknown. A young man of Bangladesh is afflicted with a strange malady. Stone-like objects resembling grains of rice come out of his eyes. All these cases are serious challenges for modern medical science. But if such an incident occurs in an area bereft of electricity, health care, science and education, it is quite natural to accept it as a curse of the evil powers.

Two cases were published in the journal *Suchetana*, edited and published by Prakash Samanta. Instead of milk, blood and pus were oozing from the udder of a cow in Dhadika village. The village heads thought that a witch had possessed the cow and called in a janguru to exorcize the evil. Nothing happened. But a veterinary doctor diagnosed the disease and explained to the people that if one sticks to the view that the cow is under an evil spell and refuses to seek the aid of a vet, then the cow loses its capacity to produce milk, which in turn would be a big loss for the owner. The same journal reports that in Brahmardiha village, south Bankura, a widow named Manada Patra had been branded a witch by the neighbouring Sinha family, and she had been beaten up. Neither the woman nor those who beat her up are tribals. All this was done only to usurp a small plot of land owned by her. The local panchayat and the police station took no steps despite complaints. The same thing happened in the case of Kaminibala Singh, an old Munda widow of Gopiballhavpur, Medinipur, West Bengal. The aim was clear—to get hold of the land owned by her.

Witch cults and the dependence on the janguru originated in the distant past. They were prevalent all over the world, not confined to the tribals. In developed countries, the beliefs have died out because of science, advancements in industry and growing prosperity. India is still languishing in the mire of underdevelopment and antiquated feudal land relations. The tribals are entangled in the cobwebs of backwardness and poverty. India is not the glamorous face which is shown on state-owned television. In the real India there is lack of drinking water and water for irrigation. In the real India famine continuously stalks the countryside. In Kalahandi, a perpetual famine situation exists for the poor tribals and they are often driven to suicide by relentless starvation. In Madhya Pradesh, thousands of poor tribals and non-tribals are turned into slaves by moneylenders and silently work for the farms owned by them. Contractors use them as slave-labourers all over India. India is the land of massacres like Arwal, Banjhi and Kansara.[6] And there is a planned

6 Arwal and Kansara were among the rural Bihar massacres repeatedly reported in 1986; Banjhi refers to the April 1985 killing of Santhals in the Santhal Parganas.

strategy to keep the real India in a state of perpetual deprivation. Millions are allocated for the development of the underdeveloped and tribal areas. If these areas attain real development, the wheel of the money game would come to a halt.

The tribals are victims of this tragedy. In view of this, is there any meaning in clinging to the witch cult in the name of keeping tribal identity and tradition alive? Everything traditional is not supportable. If the practice of sati, infanticide and the like were not abolished by law, what sort of society would we have today?

The present-day witch cult is a complex game. Many unfortunate incidents have taken place in Purulia in the period 1982–84. When the famous poet Saradaprasad Kisku and others organized a movement against witch-hunts, they immediately became targets of vicious attacks. When a recent witch killing took place, the two influential political parties claimed that the victim belonged to them and that the other party was responsible for the killing. These parties did not mount a campaign against the witch cult, did not demand punishment for the killers. They did not ask for adequate police steps. Behind the incidents of witch killing in Purulia and Singbhum are the presence of greed, political hatred, motivations of land-grabbing and extortion of money.

Nowadays, it is not only the women who are killed as witches. In *Witch Killings among Santals* (1984), A. B. Chaudhuri writes that between 1951–81, 96 witches were killed in Maldah district, several of them men. In Habibpur police station area alone, 31 women and a man were branded as witches but the police saved them. The book has the names and addresses of 15 jangurus. Regarding the killing of the 96 witches, the facts given below deserve attention. The information was brought to the police by 18 policemen, four chowkidars, two non-tribals, one panchayat president and 68 tribals; and 209 persons were convicted for the killings. But the book does not refer to punitive sentences. What is noteworthy here is the prompt action taken by the police. This has also encouraged the tribals.

From the same book, we find that a majority of the Santhals live in the Barinda area of Maldah. According to the 1981 census, the total population of Barinda is 5,01,317 of which 1,24,452 are tribals—85.35 per cent of the tribals of the district live in Barinda. During 1976–77, the per capita annual income of the tribals was Rs 555, that is Rs 34.28 per month. The per capita annual income of the district was Rs 1,047. Facilities for education are non-existent. Of the 1,30,715 tribals of Maldah, only 985 have received secondary-level education. Barinda is inaccessible during the rains and its area is 3,31,937.22 acres. The area has four primary and 10 subsidiary health centres. This means that 88,889 tribals have to depend on each centre. Apart from that, there are non-tribals. The tribals suffer from malnutrition, respiratory problems and infectious diseases. There are numerous patients of leprosy, tuberculosis and sexually transmitted diseases.

The Santhals have to survive in this cruel one-crop land. There is no irrigation, crop productivity is poor. Lack of potable water and medical facilities add to his woes. The fear of losing his land haunts him relentlessly. He cannot grasp the intricacies of the legal system and he is hounded by heartless non-tribals. This has turned the Santhals of Barinda into myopic introverts. According to law, it is forbidden to buy the land of a tribal but this law has been defeated by the khai khalasi custom. Using this custom the non-tribals grab tribal land by paying money in exchange for handwritten chits. The 1951 census shows that Santhals have lost 25,000 acres of land. The process is continuing unabated. When official records show that a Santhal owns 15 acres of land, in reality he may own only two acres. Official records fail to give the true picture since illegal land transactions are never recorded. This process is forcing the Santhal to withdraw as far away as possible from all contact with the mainstream. It is no coincidence that places where the witches are killed are generally inaccessible and cannot be reached during the rains. It is the same everywhere in West Bengal—the same life and environment. The tribals are facing increasing pressure and exploitation from the non-tribal world. Their racial identity is at stake.

In these muddy waters, the crafty sharks do everything within their means to take advantage of the ignorance of the tribals—the process of witch identification, community trial of the identified witch, fines imposed on the person and even the killing itself. In a majority of cases, the objective is to mark someone as a witch and then grab his or her land, cattle, money and even life. The political parties are afraid to take a clear stand and demand in unison—stop this damned custom! They are afraid of alienating the Santhal vote. The police also keep quiet, saying that this is an internal affair of the community.

Does the West Bengal Government really want an end to this practice? One doubts their intentions and honesty of purpose. Since positive measures have been taken by the police in West Dinajpur, the least that the government could have done is to widely publicize the measures.

But that has not been done. Why? Would the entire Santhal society turn away from the ruling parties if the government took determined steps to put a stop to this ghastly practice? Certainly not. Many Santhals, the largest tribal group in this part, are fighting against this practice as they have realized that witches are killed for the personal or political gains of a few, including the jangurus.

Let the government provide the tribals with specific programmes—both social and cultural. Santhals are culturally very alive. The tribal areas must be provided with roads, water, electricity, educational infrastructure for women, etc. Moreover, medical and natural phenomena like disease, deformed children, cattle epidemics, drought, famine should be scientifically explained through documentary films and slide lectures. Socio-economic security and spread of scientific awareness through education—both should be done simultaneously. Then you would see the Santhals coming forward to help the government.

The government should issue strict instructions to the Tribal Department and the police. Till 1981 witch killings in Maldah were treated as manslaughter. The same should be done for the rest of West Bengal. Moreover, the government must work in league with the village heads like majhis, deshmajhis, hadams, nayakes and parganas. And when the jangurus are up to any tricks, strict measures should be taken against them. Why is not a list of known jangurus being prepared and publicized, asking the people and law-enforcing agencies to keep a strict vigil on them? Change the laws, if necessary. Aren't they changed all the time to suit the interests of the ruling power and the dominant sections of the society?

In places like Maldah and Islampur the witch cult has been partly checked by the police, Tribal Department and well-meaning tribals; these are also areas where the Left Front has a strong base. But it is not utilizing the bold examples set by a section of its own administration and giving them adequate publicity. If the government fails to adopt bold policies, then who will do the job? The government should come to the aid of those who are fighting the cult. They should appoint tribals in the Tribal Department, police and homeguards in larger numbers, especially in the affected areas. The government should seek the cooperation of social development organizations working in tribal areas and also of the district newspapers.

And a lot needs to be done on the cultural front. A section of Santhal society has become vocal in support of their language and literature. This educated vanguard is fighting the witch cult. The rest of the Santhal society must also come to understand that witchcraft has mutated into something new, unlike the past—it has become the oppression of the weak by the strong and hence should be stopped. Like dowry killings, witch-hunting is also an inhuman crime. The tribals need to learn that as long as they cling to it, only the vested interests will continue to reap the benefits. The tribals are becoming victims of mainstream political conflicts and they are unaware of the funds allotted for their development by both the centre and the state. There is no awareness-generation system.

There is also the question of tribal unity. Before Independence and the politics of votes, the tribals used to have their own law and court, and their community was much more cohesive than it is today. After the hunting festival they would hold their community trials. They rarely went to the police and the courts. But that unity has broken down. They must now unite and demand that funds allocated for their development are actually spent for their benefit. I am speaking for the majority of tribals who are landless day-labourers, unemployed and jobless. Foodgrain, electricity, education, child health, medical facilities, reservation of jobs, forest preservation and afforestation, awareness about government projects—are not these more important than clinging to the leftovers of a witch cult?

I am quoting from a song which was sung during Birsa Munda's ulgulan.[7] Replace the words 'country' and 'land' by 'tribals' and you will get the correct picture.

> My country is being destroyed.
> My land is floating away
> Like turtles floating in water
> The country is in the clutches of crimson fire
> Like red leaves blooming on the tree
> My country is going to its destruction
> Land is flying away
> Like dust kicked up on the road.

I am imploring the tribals to dispassionately think about their society. I want them to question themselves—will their society progress if they keep alive the witch cult? They are being destroyed, they are floating away, they are burning like red coals in an unequal battle. In the darkness of a dust storm they are walking like ghostly slaves, walking behind the contractors, agents and touts, going to their end. They are being blown away like dust kicked up on the

---

7 Ulgulan, or 'the Great Tumult', is the name commonly used for Birsa Munda's 1899–1900 rebellion in the Chotanagpur plateau.

road. They are losing their lives, nationhood, language and culture, identity—all that there is to lose. Those who are privileged among the tribals should also think about this.

The tribals should think about who actually causes them the greater harm—those who deprive them of medicines, health, education, jobs, right to land, human rights in a free country, roads, water, irrigation—or those innocent women and men whom they brand as witches and kill? If this goes on unabated, it would be suicidal for the society.

I am quoting verbatim from a leaflet issued by a group of tribal activists against witch cult activity in Purulia—

LAW AGAINST WITCH HUNT IS NEEDED

> Even the Indian Constitution has been referring to special measures for the all-round development of the tribals, since they are backward. Santhals are numerically the majority tribals in West Bengal. The witch cult is the first among other customs which are hindering their progress.

There is no written or unwritten evidence about when and how this cult originated among the Santhals. But for a very long time, this blood-sucking unit has been crippling the Santhal society like the proverbial octopus, as a result of which the Santhal society is becoming gradually weaker. In fact, there is no such inhuman, merciless rite among the Santhals as the witch custom. Each year countless innocent and simple lives are lost, numerous hapless families are driven to destitution, many face barbaric tortures.

Countless crimes are being committed by believing the words of the hypocrite jangurus. In fact, the cult is nothing but a dark belief, a cursed superstition. It has no scientific basis whatsoever, and neither can it benefit anyone directly or indirectly. And its roots are so deep that its immediate eradication is not possible. It is a mind-boggling question how such a barbaric rite exists in a welfare state like India, even after so many years of attaining Independence. For eradication of the custom, the government should enact laws. The rite can be stopped if the janguru activity is declared illegal. We implore the state and the central government to sympathetically look at the matter and request them to enact anti-witch custom laws without delay.

Saradaprasad Kisku
President, Santhali Sahitya Parishad, Purulia

Mahadeb Hansda
Editor, *Tetre*, Santhali monthly

Kalendranath Mandi
Editor, *Sili*, bimonthly

Gurudas Murmu
Editor, *Kherwal Jharpa*

Balisrvar Saren
Editor, *Jirihiri*[8]

Age-old beliefs cannot vanish in a second. A lot of work has to be done for this. And when the beliefs go, the resultant vacuum should be filled in by education and health care for all. The social attitude to the status of women needs to be changed and an overall scientific outlook has to be developed. We must revive the bonds of love and amity, long lost, which we have replaced with hatred, greed and political violence.

The country and society have undergone big changes but our minds are still imprisoned in

8 As of 2026 India still had no central statute on witch-hunting; some states proceeded through special laws, while West Bengal was reported in 2018 to be considering its own legislation.

age-old darkness. Meaningful steps from the centre and state administrations could, perhaps, make it difficult for the cult to exist in its present form, at least. I am asking the tribals to think anew about their customs, which are hindering their development. When everywhere you are already at the receiving end, why should you yourselves kill each other? Take a look at the world at large—all the misery and crises are due to a lack of love and understanding between man and his fellow-beings. Would you like to move forward or backward? If you fail, it is you who would suffer while the vested interests would have a happy time. These forces want you to remain in darkness and fight an internecine battle over the witch issue. Will you still remain a passive victim of their evil designs?